LAW
ENFORCEMENT
AGENCIES

THE TEXAS RANGERS

LAW ENFORCEMENT AGENCIES

Bomb Squad

Border Patrol

Federal Bureau of Investigation

The Secret Service

SWAT Teams

The Texas Rangers

LAW
ENFORCEMENT
AGENCIES

THE TEXAS
RANGERS

Michael Newton

CHELSEA HOUSE
PUBLISHERS
An imprint of Infobase Publishing

THE TEXAS RANGERS

Chelsea House
An imprint of Infobase Publishing
132 West 31st Street
New York NY 10001

Library of Congress Cataloging-in-Publication Data

Newton, Michael, 1951-
The Texas Rangers / Michael Newton.
p. cm. — (Law enforcement agencies)
Includes bibliographical references and index.
ISBN-13: 978-1-60413-626-5 (hardcover : alk. paper)
ISBN-10: 1-60413-626-X (hardcover : alk. paper) 1. Texas Rangers—History. 2. Texas Rangers—Biography. 3. Law enforcement—Texas—History. I. Title.
F391.N49 2010
976.4—dc22   2010028274

Chelsea House books are available at special discounts when purchased in bulk quantities for businesses, associations, institutions, or sales promotions. Please call our Special Sales Department in New York at (212) 967-8800 or (800) 322-8755.

You can find Chelsea House on the World Wide Web at http://www.chelseahouse.com

Text design and composition by Erika K. Arroyo
Cover design by Keith Trego
Cover printed by Bang Printing, Brainerd, Minn.
Book printed and bound by Bang Printing, Brainerd, Minn.
Date printed: November 2010

Printed in the United States of America

10 9 8 7 6 5 4 3 2 1

This book is printed on acid-free paper.

All links and Web addresses were checked and verified to be correct at the time of publication. Because of the dynamic nature of the Web, some addresses and links may have changed since publication and may no longer be valid.

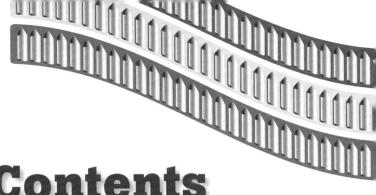

Contents

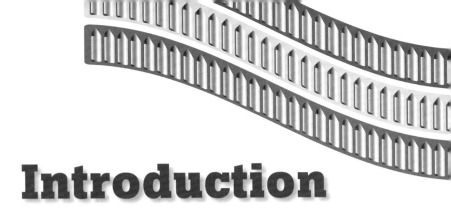

Introduction

Texas is big and proud of it. From December 1845 until January 1959, when Alaska joined the Union, Texas was the largest of the United States. And even now, in second place for size, it remains a domain of superlatives.

Texas is the only U.S. state that formerly existed as a country and the only one to join the Union by treaty, rather than territorial annexation. Flags of six nations have flown over Texas since 1635.

More land is farmed in Texas than in any other U.S. state, and Texas leads all other states in production of beef, wool, and cotton.

Texas also leads all other U.S. states in oil production and boasts the world's largest helium well, at Amarillo.

Laredo, Texas, is the world's largest inland port, while Austin claims the largest of all state capitol buildings.

Texas built America's first suspension bridge (at Waco) and its first domed stadium (in Houston).

In terms of natural wonders, Texas claims more species of bats, reptiles, and wildflowers than any other U.S. state. It also has the country's largest herd of whitetail deer.

America's worst-ever natural disaster occurred at Galveston in September 1900, when a hurricane killed at least 6,000 persons (with some reports claiming 12,000).[1]

It is only natural, therefore, that Texas should also spawn one of the world's most famous law enforcement agencies. After the Federal Bureau of Investigation (FBI)—and, perhaps, the Royal Canadian Mounted Police—no police force on Earth is better known than the Texas Rangers. And few are older. While the FBI dates its history from 1908, and the Mounties were not organized until 1920, the first Texas

Rangers saddled up for action in 1823, six years before London's Metropolitan Police and 15 years before Boston established America's first city police department.

During their long, turbulent history the Texas Rangers have served, by turns, as soldiers (fighting Indians, Mexican troops, and even the United States), as frontier guardsmen, as strikebreakers, and as manhunters pursuing some of the nation's most dangerous fugitives. They have grappled with corruption and sometimes surrendered to it, enduring scandal and rising above it, to stand as near-mythical heroes in fact and fiction. The Texas Ranger Hall of Fame includes gunfighters and martyrs, hard-riding frontiersmen, and combatants in the modern war

The Texas Ranger Hall of Fame and Museum in Waco, Texas, consists of the Homer Garrison Jr. museum gallery, the Texas Ranger Hall of Fame, the Texas Ranger Research Center, and the Headquarters of Texas Ranger Company F. (NY Daily News *via Getty Images*)

on crime. Since 1837, at least 103 Rangers have lost their lives in the line of duty.[2]

The Texas Rangers also rank among the law enforcement agencies most frequently portrayed in fiction and on film. Countless novels depicting Ranger exploits have been published since the first one appeared in 1856, later spawning radio and television series aired worldwide. Between 1910 and 2007, fictional Rangers appeared as major characters in 222 motion pictures.[3]

The Texas Rangers traces the history of America's premiere law enforcement agency from its beginnings on the wild, lawless frontier to its performance in the modern world of drugs, terrorism, organized crime, and serial murder.

Chapter 1, "Early Rangers," traces Ranger history from the appointment of its first members in 1823, through reorganization as a 25-man force in 1835, to the admission of Texas as a U.S. state 10 years later.

Chapter 2, "Patrolling the Frontier," proceeds from the early challenges and frontier wars of statehood, through secession, Civil War, and Reconstruction, climaxed by Texas's readmission to the Union in January 1874.

Chapter 3, "The Late 19th Century," charts Ranger history from the creation of six new companies in May 1874 through the end of the 19th century.

Chapter 4, "Lawless Years," details the troubled years from 1901 through 1934, as the Rangers struggled with oil booms and Mexican revolutionaries, political corruption during Prohibition's "noble experiment," and violent bank-robbing gangs spawned by the Great Depression.

Chapter 5, "A New Department," picks up with creation of the Texas Department of Public Safety in 1935 and continues through the 1960s, examining Ranger duties related to World War II, labor violence, and the turmoil surrounding pursuit of civil rights for African Americans.

Chapter 6, "Modern Problems," examines Ranger responses to crime in a new age, including prison riots, drug wars, investigation of ransom kidnappings, and pursuit of nomadic serial killers.

Chapter 7, "Ranger Heroes," chronicles the lives of the most famous Texas Rangers throughout history, presenting their best-known adventures, analyzing their contributions to the agency, and some of the controversies they inspired.

Chapter 8, "Fictional Rangers," tracks the depiction of Rangers who never were, through magazines and novels, radio, film, and television, from 1856 to the present.

Early Rangers

November 10, 1837

After four weeks in the saddle, Captain William Eastland's company of Texas Rangers was ready for battle. Their long search had begun on October 13, after a war party of Kichai Indians raided Fort Smith, on the Little River. Eastland's party had pursued the raiders, then lost the trail and divided their force to broaden the search. Seventeen Rangers, led by Lieutenant A.B. Van Benthusen, picked up the raiders' trail on November 1, and killed one Kichai tribesman two days later, near the future site of Fort Belknap. On November 10 they found 150 Kichais massed and waiting in present-day Archer County, at a place the tribe called "Stone Houses," after a nearby rock formation.

Friendly Cherokee and Delaware Indians tried to negotiate peace before Ranger Felix McClusky shot and killed one of the Kichai tribesmen without apparent provocation. The rest then attacked, while Lt. Van Benthusen's men abandoned their horses, dodging arrows and bullets, to find cover in a shallow ravine. Rangers killed the war party's chief in the first attack, but the Kichai fought on, slaying four Rangers, then setting fire to the prairie around them. The surviving Rangers charged through smoke and flames, losing six more men before they finally escaped on foot and hiked back to the nearest settlement, arriving at last on November 27.

Lieutenant Van Benthusen and Felix McClusky survived the Battle of Stone Houses. Those lost included Second Lieutenant Alfred Miles and nine privates: Jesse Blair, Alexander Bostwick, James Christian, Joseph Cooper, James Joslen, Westley Nicholson, William Nicholson, William Sanders, and Lewis Scheuster. A historic marker was erected to their memory in 1970, located 10 miles south of Windthorst, in Archer County.

COLONIAL RANGERS

Moses Austin (1761–1821) was a man of vision. Born in Connecticut, he pioneered America's lead-mining industry in the 1790s, founded the Bank of St. Louis in 1815, and then hatched a plan to plant an American colony in Spanish Texas. Spanish authorities granted permission in December 1820, but Austin caught pneumonia during the negotiations and died in June 1821, after obtaining son Stephen's promise to pursue "the Texas Venture."[1] Three months later, Mexico won independence from Spain, after 11 years of armed conflict. Mexico's new government allowed Stephen Austin to launch his father's colony, provided that new settlers spoke Spanish, adopted the Catholic religion, and became Mexican citizens.

The first settlers arrived in 1822 and soon met violent opposition from native Comanche, Karankawa, Tehuacani, Tonkawa, and Waco tribesmen. In May 1823, Austin's lieutenant Moses Morrison organized a small self-defense force. Three months later, Austin himself formed a second group of "ten men. . .to act as rangers for the common defense," a dangerous job that paid 15 dollars per month "in property."[2]

The first *rangers*—literally, those who range (travel) over wide areas—were 14th-century British gamekeepers, assigned to guard the King of England's forest property and wildlife. By 1823, the term applied to law enforcement officers or soldiers whose domain was mostly wilderness. One observer described Austin's rangers by saying, "They ride like a Mexican, trail like an Indian, shoot like a Tennesseean, and fight like the devil."[3] Early Texas Rangers served tours of duty ranging from days to months, as needed, and their pay was often slow in coming, when it came at all. With or without a steady paycheck, they furnished their own horses, weapons, and all other equipment required to survive on the range.

The Texas–Indian Wars of 1823–1836 were chaotic and brutal, including violence between rival tribes and occasional confusion that

In a gathering of colonists in 1823 on the Colorado River, not far from the present day town of Bay City, Texas, Stephen F. Austin *(right, in dark coat)* and Baron de Bastrop *(seated),* Land Commissioner of the Mexican Government, issue land to colonists. *(Bettmann/Corbis)*

produced Ranger attacks on "friendly" Indians. Mexico's government made matters worse by signing, then breaking various treaties, while offering cash bounties for Indian scalps. Angry tribesmen punished Texans for the actions of politicians in Mexico City, and Rangers retaliated without mercy.

One such incident was the Fort Parker massacre of May 1836. Fort Parker was a civilian stronghold and trading post, named for the family that built it in 1834. Elder John Parker allowed Texas Rangers to use his settlement as a base for raids against Comanche and Kiowa Indians, which enraged the tribesmen. On May 19 a mixed war party of Comanches, Delaware, Kiowa, and Wichitas stormed Fort Parker, killing five settlers, kidnapping two women and three children. Rangers searched in vain for the captives, before they were distracted by a war with Mexico. Both women and one of the children were ransomed, but two captive children spent most of their lives among the Comanche. Their experience inspired a classic Western film, *The Searchers*, released in 1956.

Matters went from bad to worse as Mexico tightened its control over Texas, refusing an American offer to buy Texas for $5 million in 1829, finally banning new immigration from the United States in April

STEPHEN FULLER AUSTIN

The "Father of Texas"—and of the Texas Rangers—was born in Virginia on November 3, 1793. His family moved to Missouri in 1798, later sending Stephen to school in Connecticut and Kentucky. He later served as a militia officer and member of Missouri's territorial legislature, then as a circuit judge in Arkansas. His father's death, in 1821, left Austin to fulfill the family's passion for foundation of a colony in Texas. By 1823, he had secured a promise of land grants for 300 families from the United States, later increased to 900—a deal that also granted Austin 67,000 acres for each family he lured to Texas.

Mexico's government granted Austin full authority over his colonists, but he used it judiciously, permitting election of local mayors and militia officers. As a lieutenant colonel of the Texas militia, he planned campaigns against hostile Indian tribes and created the first Ranger troop for frontier defense. Austin also promoted surveying to end land disputes and lobbied for legalization of slavery. Mexican leaders agreed, then changed their minds and banned slavery in 1829, lighting the fuse for rebellion among Texas slave owners.

When Mexico banned further U.S. immigration in April 1830, Austin launched a campaign that overturned the ban

1830. Armed clashes between "Texians" and Mexican troops began in June 1832, with the Battle of Velasco. Mexican troops arrested Stephen Austin in April 1833, on charges of inciting revolution, and held him in prison until July 1835.

"COME AND TAKE IT!"

In 1834, with several Mexican states in open revolt, President Antonio López de Santa Anna declared himself dictator, suspended Mexico's democratic constitution, and prepared to crush his opponents. To pacify Texans, Santa Anna freed Stephen Austin and then sent troops

in December 1833. Still, it was too late to douse the flames of unrest in Texas. Austin was jailed in April 1833, for leading a convention to discuss independence, and he remained in custody until July 1835. During 1836, while Texans fought Mexican troops for their freedom, Austin negotiated U.S. recognition of the fledgling Lone Star Republic, finally secured on March 3, 1837.

Stephen Austin did not live to witness that final victory. Defeated in his September 1836 campaign to become first president of Texas, he agreed to serve as secretary of state under winner Sam Houston. Two months later, on December 27, Austin died from pneumonia—the same disease that claimed his father's life—at age 43, in Columbia, Texas. His life's work is best summarized in Austin's own words, penned in July 1836: "The prosperity of Texas has been the object of my labors, the idol of my existence—it has assumed the character of a religion, for the guidance of my thoughts and actions, for fifteen years."[4]

Austin's memory lives on in modern Texas. The state's capital bears his name, as do Austin County, Stephen F. Austin State University in Nacogdoches, Austin College in Sherman, plus more than a dozen local schools.

Texas settlers and Mexican President Antonio López de Santa Anna's forces do battle at the Alamo in San Antonio, Texas. A total of 167 settlers died in the battle. *(Bettmann/Corbis)*

to seize a cannon owned by U.S. immigrants at Gonzales. The settlers raised a defiant banner reading "Come and Take It." One week later, on October 9, 1835, Texas volunteers captured a Mexican fort at Goliad.

The Texas Revolution had begun.

Colonists organized a provisional government on November 3, 1835, creating a 25-man "Corps of Rangers" under R.M. Williamson to guard the frontier. Later expanded to three companies of 56 men each, the Rangers earned $1.25 per day and were empowered to elect their own officers, including Captains William Arrington, Isaac Burleson, and John Tumlinson. Loose organization made it difficult to say which revolutionary fighters were Texas Rangers and which belonged to the larger "Texian Army."

In December 1835 Texas forces drove Santa Anna's brother-in-law, General Martín Perfecto de Cos, from his garrison at San Antonio. Santa Anna led his army north in January 1836 to punish the colonists, many of whom fled their homes under guard by Captain John Tumlinson's Rangers, in an exodus nicknamed the "Runaway Scrape." Meanwhile, 22 members of the Gonzales Ranging Company of Mounted Volunteers joined Colonel William Travis at the Alamo, in San Antonio, and died with 167 others when Santa Anna's army seized the fort on March 6.

That massacre, while relatively minor in comparison with other famous battles, enflamed all of Texas. Santa Anna's slaughter of every man found in the fortress—including seven who surrendered—sparked unrelenting hatred of the general. Heroic images were also fostered by the Alamo's "celebrity" defenders, including Colonel Travis, Tennessee frontiersman David "Davy" Crockett, and James Bowie, a wealthy Texan notorious for dueling with pistols and the Bowie knife that he invented sometime in the mid-1820s.

Texan rage increased three weeks later, when Santa Anna massacred 350 prisoners of war at Goliad. General Sam Houston avenged that loss and secured independence for Texas on April 21, when he defeated Santa Anna at the Battle of San Jacinto. Mexico acknowledged Texas as a free republic, with Houston elected president in October 1836. Five months later, the United States recognized the Republic of Texas.

DEFENDING THE FRONTIER

Santa Anna's defeat brought no peace to Texas. Bloody conflict with various Indian tribes, border guerrillas, and Mexican troops continued for the next eight years. During 1838–1841, President Mirabeau Lamar sent three agents to Mexico requesting peace, but all three missions failed. In May 1839 a captured diplomatic letter revealed Mexico's plan to enlist hostile Indian tribes in attacks throughout Texas. President Lamar retaliated with a plan to drive all Native tribesmen out of Texas, starting with the Cherokees.

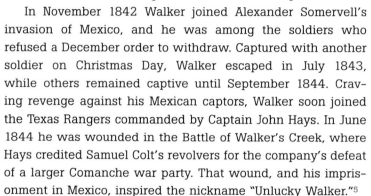

SAMUEL HAMILTON WALKER

Sam Walker was born in Maryland, on February 24, 1817. At age 19 he left the carpentry trade to join a militia company bound for action in Florida's Second Seminole War. Discharged in 1838, he next worked on a railroad, then surfaced in Galveston, Texas, during January 1842. Nine months later, as a member of Captain Jesse Billingsley's Mounted Volunteers, Walker helped repel General Adrian Woll's troops at the Battle of Salado Creek, defeating Mexico's bid to reconquer Texas.

In November 1842 Walker joined Alexander Somervell's invasion of Mexico, and he was among the soldiers who refused a December order to withdraw. Captured with another soldier on Christmas Day, Walker escaped in July 1843, while others remained captive until September 1844. Craving revenge against his Mexican captors, Walker soon joined the Texas Rangers commanded by Captain John Hays. In June 1844 he was wounded in the Battle of Walker's Creek, where Hays credited Samuel Colt's revolvers for the company's defeat of a larger Comanche war party. That wound, and his imprisonment in Mexico, inspired the nickname "Unlucky Walker."[5]

Discharged from the Texas Rangers in September 1845, Walker immediately joined a new unit, the Texas Mounted

That tribe had been promised full title to their East Texas land in 1836, if they remained neutral during the Texas Revolution against Mexico, but the Texas senate nullified that treaty in December 1837, over Sam Houston's objections. In 1839, when Lamar ordered the Cherokee to leave Texas and move to the Indian Territory (now Oklahoma), they angrily refused. On July 12, 1839, Texas militia officers made a new deal with the Cherokee. The tribe agreed to leave Texas if they were compensated for their travel cost and crops already planted for that year. They balked at leaving under armed guard, however, which prompted a July 15 militia attack on a village of Cherokees, Delaware, and Shawnee tribesmen, led by 83-year-old Chief Bowl (or Bold Hunter).

Rangers. He later borrowed that name for a volunteer company that he formed in April 1846 for combat in the Mexican War. That service—including a false report of his death in battle—elevated Walker to second-in-command of the Texas Mounted Riflemen, under Colonel John Hays. The first phase of Walker's war ended with his discharge, in October 1846, but he rebounded by recruiting a new group of volunteers in New York.

While there, Walker met Samuel Colt and suggested improvements to Colt's original revolver, including the addition of a sixth chamber and a trigger guard to prevent accidental firing. The new .44-caliber pistol, known as the 1847 Walker Colt, reigned as the world's most powerful commercially produced handgun until 1935, when the .357 Magnum was invented.

Captain Walker's Company C of the First United States Mounted Rifles received their first shipment of Walker Colts at Vera Cruz, in June 1847, but the guns were warehoused and did not reach Walker's troops in time to save his life. On October 9 Walker died in battle against Mexican guerrillas at Huamantla. The army shipped his body back to San Antonio for burial. Today, he is an honored member of the Texas Ranger Hall of Fame.

The so-called Battle of the Neches was an uneven match. Although Chief Bowl's tribesmen outnumbered the militia forces 800 to 500, they suffered 100 deaths, while only three militiamen were killed in two days of fighting. Chief Bowl, when slain, wore a sword and sash presented to him by Sam Houston, three years earlier. Soldiers burned Cherokee crops and pursued surviving tribesmen for a week, until the survivors escaped into Arkansas. The attack sparked several months of conflict. A final clash on December 25, 1839, near the San Saba River, killed Chief Egg and several warriors, while 27 Cherokee women and children were captured. Thus ended the Cherokee War.

Meanwhile, Comanche raiders ravaged the Texas frontier. In March 1840 Texas troops killed 38 tribal leaders during peace negotiations at San Antonio. More raiding followed, climaxing on August 11 with the Battle of Plum Creek, where Ben McCulloch's Texas Rangers and volunteer militiamen defeated a large Comanche force and drove its survivors westward.

Cross-border raiding by Mexican troops resumed in March 1842, including strikes at Goliad, San Antonio, and Victoria. General Adrian Woll occupied San Antonio with 1,500 men on September 11 and rashly declared Texas reconquered by Mexico. Two hundred volunteers, including 14 Rangers led by Captain Jack Hays, lured Woll's army into the Battle of Salado Creek on September 18, defeating the invaders and forcing their retreat to Mexico.

Emboldened by that victory, in October 1842 Texas militia crossed the Nueces River onto land still owned by Mexico. Commander Alexander Somervell abandoned the campaign on December 19, but only 189 of his 497 men obeyed the order to retreat. The rest—including Rangers Ben McCulloch and William "Big Foot" Wallace—pushed on to Ciudad Mier, where they clashed with Mexican troops. Thirty Texans and 600 Mexicans died before the Texans ran short of ammunition and surrendered. Seventeen prisoners were executed, while others died in captivity. Some, including McCulloch, escaped. The survivors were released in September 1844.

Back in Texas, conflict with Comanche tribesmen had resumed. Armed with deadly five-shot Colt revolvers, Texas Rangers led by Captain John Hays fought many frontier skirmishes against warriors led by Chiefs Buffalo Hump and Yellow Wolf. When armed clashes at Plum Creek, Cañon de Ugalde, Bandera Pass, Painted Rock, and Salado failed to stop the Comanche attacks, Hays determined to end the war once and for all.

On June 1, 1844, Hays left his San Antonio headquarters with 14 Rangers, searching for Yellow Wolf's raiders. Eight days later, in present-day Kendall County, Hays faced a war party including at least 40 Comanches; some reports claimed 200. Yellow Wolf concealed most of his men, exposing a few as bait for an ambush, taunting Hays and his Rangers with insults. Suspicious, Hays led his men in a flanking attack, resulting in hand-to-hand combat described as "rough and tumble" by participant Ben McCulloch.[6]

Two counterattacks failed to break the Rangers, and Yellow Wolf's Comanches fled, pursued for three miles by their enemies while Major Hays shouted, "Crowd them! Powder-burn them!" Ranger losses totaled one man killed and four seriously wounded, all of whom survived. The *Houston Daily Star* described the Battle of Walker's Creek—also confusingly known as the Battle of Asta's Creek, the Battle of Sisters Creek, and the Battle of Pinta Tail Crossing—as "unparalleled in this country for the gallantry displayed on both sides, its close and deadly struggle, and the triumphant success of the gallant partisan captain of the West [Hays]." A Comanche survivor later explained the victory of 14 men against 40 (or 200) by recalling that the Rangers "had a shot for every finger on the hand" with their revolvers.[7]

As a result of Yellow Wolf's defeat, the Comanches and other hostile tribes entered peace negotiations with Sam Houston, then serving his second term as president of Texas. The final treaty, signed on October 9, 1844, included a cease-fire with the Comanches, Anadarkos, Caddos, Delawares, Hainais, Kichais, Lipan Apaches, Shawnees, Tawakonis, and Wacos. Sadly, as with other treaties made before and afterward, it would not guarantee eternal peace.

FROM NATION TO STATE

Despite a failed attempt to buy Texas from Mexico in 1829, the United States still hoped to expand by acquiring the Lone Star Republic. President John Tyler (1790–1862) signed a treaty of annexation in April 1844, ignoring Santa Anna's warning that absorption of Texas would be "equivalent to a declaration of war" against Mexico, but the U.S. Senate rejected that treaty in June, by a vote of 35 to 16.[8]

Five months later, James Polk (1795–1849) won election to the White House with a campaign promise to expand the country. Polk avoided confrontation with the Senate over treaties by promoting a joint resolution of Congress to annex Texas. The resolution passed in February 1845, with a two-vote margin of victory in the Senate, and Polk sent diplomat Andrew Donelson to seek approval from Texas. Lone Star president Anson Jones convened the Texas Congress in

June 1845 and secured a vote of confirmation. Texan voters ratified a new state constitution in October 1845, which was approved by Congress two months later. Although Texas formally joined the Union on December 29, 1845, formal conversion from republic to state occurred on February 16, 1846, when President Jones surrendered authority to Governor James Henderson.

By that time, Mexico had severed diplomatic relations with the United States. Another war was brewing, and the Texas Rangers would be in the thick of it.

Patrolling
the Frontier

August 20, 1850

In May of 1850, Texas Rangers D.C. "Doc" Sullivan, Alpheus Neill, and John Wilbarger requested leave from their company to deal with private legal matters. Despite ongoing clashes with Comanche warriors that had claimed the life of Ranger William Gillespie on May 29, Captain John Ford gave the trio 90 days to finish their business and report back for duty. On August 20, Sullivan, Neill, and Wilbarger met at San Antonio Viejo, in present-day Jim Hogg County, to begin their homeward journey.

They were not alone.

Before traveling far, the Rangers noted a party of 30 Comanches following them. Instead of trying to outrun the warriors, they chose to stand and fight. One of the Comanches fired a rifle shot that pierced Doc Sullivan's body, knocking him from his saddle. Neill and Wilbarger dragged him to a nearby tree and bound him sitting upright, with a rope, but it was hopeless. "I am killed," Sullivan told his friends. "You can do me no good. Make your escape."[1] Just then, another bullet struck him in the head and finished him.

Instead of fleeing, John Wilbarger charged the Indians, firing his Colt revolver, dropping two or three warriors before he was killed. Alpheus Neill fell from his horse, which bolted and was captured by the tribesmen, with his weapons on the saddle. Unarmed and afoot, Neill collapsed after being shot eight times with rifles and bows. The Comanches stripped him and left him for dead—but he lived.

Hours later, Neill woke, pulled several arrows from his flesh, and set off naked through the desert to find help. Walking and crawling by turns, he finally reached San Patricio, 65 miles from the scene of the battle, where settlers bound his wounds and rode out to retrieve John Wilbarger's body. Doc Sullivan's corpse was never found.

Alpheus Neill later retired from the Texas Rangers, to become a policeman in Waco, Texas. He was shot and killed while investigating a family quarrel on February 6, 1877.

"TEXAS DEVILS"

The seeds of war between America and Mexico were sown before Texas joined the Union. President Polk hoped to expand the United States from coast to coast, and he wasted no time in pursuing that goal. Polk sent General Zachary Taylor to Texas in June 1845, and by October, 3,500 American troops were massed along the Nueces River, which Mexico claimed was the southern boundary of Texas. Texans insisted that their land extended to the Rio Grande, 150 miles farther south. In November, Polk offered Mexico $25 million ($620 million today) for the remainder of Texas, plus the area of present-day California, Arizona, and New Mexico.

Mexico refused that offer and severed diplomatic relations with the United States a month later, when Congress annexed Texas. Militant leaders unseated President José Joaquín de Herrera in January 1846, after five days in office, and replaced him with General Mariano Paredes, who opposed America's territorial demands. American diplomat John Slidell recommended that Mexico be "chastised" by force.[2]

President Polk agreed, ordering General Taylor to cross the Nueces River. On April 25, 1846, Mexican cavalry killed 11 members of a U.S. patrol in the disputed region. Two weeks later, claiming that "Mexico has passed the boundary of the United States, has invaded our territory and shed American blood upon American soil," President Polk convinced Congress to declare war on Mexico.[3] Mexico did not follow until July 7, after the U.S. Navy occupied Monterey, California. By that time, American troops had defeated Mexican forces in four engagements and had occupied Matamoros.

With the formal outbreak of hostilities, three regiments of Texas Rangers joined the U.S. Army under the command of Texas Governor J. Pinckney Henderson. Military historian Robert Leckie notes that "[t] here had been little time to furnish them all with military uniforms, so that they were on the whole a villainous-looking lot, long-haired, bearded and mustachioed in an age when most men—especially soldiers—cut their hair and were clean-shaven. They could be identified

In the agency's early days, Texas Rangers did not have uniforms and were characterized by their rugged appearance. *(Bettmann/ Corbis)*

by their wide-brimmed slouch hats—akin to the Mexican sombrero—that they wore and the belt of pistols at their waists."[4]

Ranger tactics matched their rough appearance, battling so fiercely that their Mexican opponents called them "packs of human blood-hounds" and *Los Diablos Tejanos*—"the Texas Devils."[5] An example of their methods was described in newspaper reports of an attack on a ranch near Agua Fria.

> The place was surrounded, the doors forced in and all the males capable of bearing arms were dragged out, tied to a post and shot! ... Thirty-six Mexicans were shot at this place, a half hour given for the horrified survivors, women and children, to remove their little household goods, then the torch was applied to the houses and by the light of the conflagration the ferocious *Tejanos* rode off to fresh scenes of blood.[6]

Compared to the damage they inflicted, Rangers serving with the army seem to have avoided major losses. The Texas Ranger Hall of Fame lists only six Rangers slain—all killed in battle at Port Isabel, on April 28, 1846—but at least two others were omitted from the list. Captain Robert Gillespie fell in the Battle of Monterey, on September 22, 1846, while Captain Sam "Unlucky" Walker died while leading a charge of the U.S. Mounted Rifles in the Battle of Huamantla, on October 9, 1847. Army casualty lists for the Mexican War include one Texas Ranger wounded, plus one killed and five wounded among the Texas Mounted Volunteers.[7]

The Treaty of Guadalupe Hidalgo, signed on February 3, 1848, ended the war and granted America all it had asked for three years earlier, at lower rates. With the stroke of a pen, the United States acquired 525,000 square miles of new land—55 percent of Mexico's pre-war domain—for a total cost of $18 million ($381 million today).[8] Press coverage of the Texas Rangers sent them home as heroes, ready to confront new challenges.

OLD ENEMIES, NEW BATTLES

Diversion of the Texas Rangers into military service during 1846–1848 left the frontier unguarded. Indian raids continued and outlaws

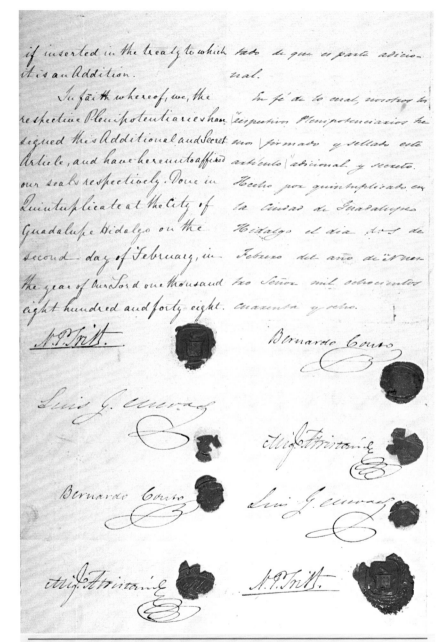

The Treaty of Guadalupe Hidalgo ended the Mexican–American War and added a vast amount of territory to the United States. Mexico relinquished all claims to the territory of Texas above the Rio Grande and ceded New Mexico and California to the United States in exchange for $15 million. *(Hulton-Deutsch Collection/Corbis)*

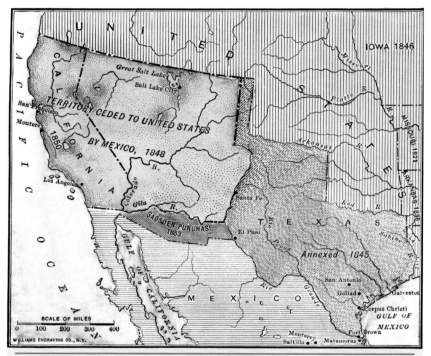

After the Mexican–American War, Mexico gave 525,000 square miles of territory to the United States. From the standpoint of Mexico, the cession included an additional 389,166 miles as Mexico never recognized the Republic of Texas nor annexation by the United States in 1945. In total, Mexico lost 55 percent of its pre-war territory. *(North Wind Picture Archives via AP Images)*

abounded, terrorizing Texas residents. A congressional report from 1848 declared: "Many were murdered, others robbed of all they possessed, and a general fear and alarm diffused throughout the whole of the frontier."[9]

The solution: more Texas Rangers.

On November 16, 1848, an editorial in the *Victoria* (Texas) *Advocate* announced that "Four newly raised ranging companies have all been organized, and taken their several stations on our frontier. We are much pleased. We know they are true men; and they know exactly what they are about. With many of them Indian and Mexican fighting has been their trade for years. That they may be permanently retained in the service on our frontier is extremely desirable; and we cannot permit ourselves to doubt but such will be the case."[10] Two more companies were organized in 1849.

Over the next decade, Rangers battled outlaws and Indians alike, upholding their reputation for rough-and-ready action. Their most famous leader of the era was John Ford (1815–1897), nicknamed "R.I.P."—"Rest in Peace"—for the letters he had penned to families of Texas volunteers killed in the Mexican War.[11] Appointed as a Ranger captain in 1849, Ford patrolled the troubled region between the Nueces and Rio Grande rivers, operating from headquarters at San Antonio Viejo.

Ford left the Rangers in 1852 to serve in the Texas state senate while running an Austin newspaper, but he returned to active duty in 1858, when Indian raiding resumed. At sunrise on May 12 of that year, Ford led 102 Rangers and 113 Brazos Reservation Indians against a large Comanche force under Chief Iron Jacket, camped on the South Canadian River. The resultant Battle of Little Robe Creek spanned most of the day, including defeat of Comanche reinforcements who arrived late on the scene. Three Texans died in the fighting, with five more wounded, while Ford's troops killed Iron Jacket and 75 other Comanches, wounded an uncertain number who escaped, and captured 18 stragglers plus 300 Comanche horses.[12]

Afterward, Ford was accused of targeting Comanche women and children, to which he replied that it was difficult to tell "warriors from squaws." Other critics claimed that Ford and his Rangers allowed their Indian allies to mutilate and eat the dead Comanches, using severed hands and feet to decorate their saddles. In private, Ford apparently told racist jokes suggesting that he did not care about the age or sex of Indians his Rangers killed.[13] Such attitudes were common in the 19th century, when savage frontier warfare frequently brought out the worst in both sides.

Next to stir the boiling pot was Juan Cortina (1824–1894), a Mexican bandit and folk hero, twice indicted for rustling cattle in Cameron County but saved from arrest by Mexican Americans who admired him. In July 1859, after Brownsville's city marshal beat and jailed one of Cortina's friends, Cortina shot the lawman and freed the prisoner.

Two months later, on September 28, Cortina returned to Brownsville with at least 40 gunmen, shot five Anglos, then rode through the

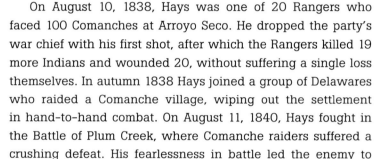

JOHN COFFEE HAYS (1817–1883)

John Hays, generally known as "Jack," was a Tennessee native who studied surveying at age 15, then moved to Texas in 1836, soon after the Alamo's fall. He joined the Texas militia and helped bury victims of the Goliad massacre, then enlisted with a company of Rangers led by Erastus "Deaf" Smith, pursuing outlaws and skirmishing with Mexican cavalry along the Lone Star Republic's disputed border.

On August 10, 1838, Hays was one of 20 Rangers who faced 100 Comanches at Arroyo Seco. He dropped the party's war chief with his first shot, after which the Rangers killed 19 more Indians and wounded 20, without suffering a single loss themselves. In autumn 1838 Hays joined a group of Delawares who raided a Comanche village, wiping out the settlement in hand-to-hand combat. On August 11, 1840, Hays fought in the Battle of Plum Creek, where Comanche raiders suffered a crushing defeat. His fearlessness in battle led the enemy to dub Hays "Devil Yack."[14]

Such exploits saw Hays promoted to sergeant, then captain and major. On July 1, 1841, he led 12 Rangers in pursuit of Comanches at Uvalde Canyon, where an arrow severed one of his fingers. Later engagements included battles fought at Cañon de Ugalde, Bandera Pass, Painted Rock, Salado, and

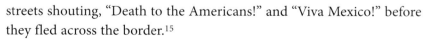

streets shouting, "Death to the Americans!" and "Viva Mexico!" before they fled across the border.[15]

So began the "Cortina War." On September 30 Cortina announced plans to punish anyone who abused Mexicans residing in Texas. Anglo residents calling themselves the "Brownsville Tigers" joined Mexican militiamen from nearby Matamoros to raid Cortina's ranch in Cameron County, but Cortina drove them off and threatened to burn Brownsville if one of his men, jailed there for murder, was not released. Anglo authorities hanged the prisoner instead. On November 23 Cortina asked Governor Sam Houston to defend the rights of Mexican Americans in Texas.

Walker's Creek. During the Mexican War of 1846–1848, Hays led the First Regiment of Texas Mounted Riflemen, scouting for General Zachary Taylor and participating in battles at Monterrey, Nuevo Leon, Teotihuacán, and Sequalteplán. When not engaged in active combat, Hays and his men guarded critical army supply lines between Veracruz and Mexico City.

In 1849 the California gold rush lured Hays away from Texas. He was elected sheriff of San Francisco County in 1850, was promoted to serve as California's Surveyor General in 1853, and helped found the present-day city of Oakland, where his investments included banks, real estate, and utilities. In 1860, after Paiute raiders killed 46 Nevada militiamen, Hays organized the Washoe Regiment—described by Ranger historian Bill O'Neal as "a collection of somewhat unsavory citizens"—and defeated the hostiles at the Battle of Big Meadows, where Hays once again shot the war chief. On June 2, 1860, Hays led 300 men against 800 Paiutes, killing 30 and capturing 50 families, against militia losses of 11 men.[16]

That was Hays's last engagement on a battlefield. He never returned to Texas, conducting his life of finance and politics from an 800-acre ranch at Fernwood, California. Hays served as a delegate to the Democratic National Convention in 1876 and died on April 21, 1883. His last words were, "It's San Jacinto Day!"[17]

Ignoring that message, Houston sent troops, including John Ford's Rangers and 165 militia regulars. Cortina, with an estimated 400 men on his side, met that force on December 27, at Rio Grande City, and was soundly defeated, losing 60 of his men and most of his equipment.[18] He retreated into Mexico, but soon resumed raiding across the border, operating from the rugged Burgos Mountains.

On December 18, 1860, Ranger captain and future Texas governor John Ross led his men in a dawn raid against a band of Comanches camped beside the Pease River, in present-day Foard County. Most of the Indians present were slain, though historians disagree on the fate of

Chief Peta Nocona. Ross claimed to have killed Nocona, but Nocona's son later claimed that Nocona missed the raid and died from smallpox with his other son in 1863. As in many battles of the era, women and children were killed along with warriors. The only known survivors were Cynthia Parker (kidnapped in the Fort Parker massacre of 1836 and later married to Peta Nocona), her daughter Topasannah ("Prairie Flower"), and an unidentified 10-year-old boy saved by Captain Ross. Cynthia Parker was placed under guard, to prevent her rejoining the Comanches, but she never adjusted to life in white society. Topasannah

"BIG FOOT" WALLACE (1817–1899)

William Alexander Anderson Wallace was born in Virginia, a descendant of Scottish warrior William Wallace, portrayed by Mel Gibson in the Oscar-winning film *Braveheart* (1995). He moved to Texas in 1836, to "take pay out of the Mexicans" after two of his cousins died in the Goliad massacre.[19] He joined the company of Texas Rangers led by Captain John Hays in March 1842 and was among the troops who expelled General Adrian Woll from San Antonio three months later. In December 1842 Wallace joined the Somervell expedition and was captured with others at Ciudad Mier. Spared from execution by a lottery, he was released in September 1844.

One story claims that Wallace got his "Big Foot" nickname from Mexican jailers, who could not find shoes to fit him, but Wallace denied that claim, noting that despite his six-foot-two-inch stature and 240 pounds, his feet were a standard size 10. Wallace claimed he earned the nickname because he wore moccasins resembling those favored by a Waco Indian warrior called "Big Foot," whose footprints were found at a raided homestead. The ranch's owner first accused Wallace of looting his home, but Wallace cleared himself by proving that his feet were smaller than the Waco's. Still, the nickname stuck for the remainder of his life.[20]

Parker died from pneumonia in 1864, followed by her mother in 1870 or 1871. Different reports blame Cynthia Parker's death on influenza or starvation from a hunger strike.[21]

CONFEDERATE RANGERS

In 1860 Texas was one of 15 states that permitted slavery; 18 others had banned human bondage between 1787 and 1859. November's election of President Abraham Lincoln—who pledged to bar slavery from all future states—sparked fury and panic among wealthy slave owners.

Wallace rejoined the Texas Rangers in December 1845, serving in the Mexican War under Captains John Hays and Robert Gillespie. In September 1846, Wallace participated as a first lieutenant in the Battle of Monterrey, where Gillespie was killed as they stormed the Bishop's Palace, on Independence Hill.

In 1849, as captain of his own Ranger company, Wallace pursued Comanches from headquarters at Fort Clark, then retired in 1850 to guard U.S. mail shipments between El Paso and San Antonio. He also collected bounties for capturing runaway slaves under the controversial Fugitive Slave Act passed by Congress in September 1850. (At the time, pursuit of runaways was standard procedure for Southern law enforcement officers.) Governor Peter Bell next persuaded Wallace to lead a group of 76 Texas Rangers patrolling the state's southwestern frontier, where Wallace engaged in more Indian battles. He remained on duty through the Civil War, expanding his patrols to track Confederate deserters and skirmish with Union invaders.

Little is known of Wallace's post-war life, but 1874 found him living in Frio County, near a town named "Bigfoot" in his honor. In 1898 he dictated his memoirs to Ranger-turned-author A.J. Sowell, then died on January 7, 1899, at age 81. Noting that Wallace never married, a speaker at his funeral declared that his "whole life was sacrificed to duty."[22]

Between December 1860 and June 1861, 11 southern states seceded from the Union. Texas was seventh in line, officially leaving the United States on March 1, 1861, to join the newly formed Confederate States of America.

During the Civil War that followed (1861–1865), thousands of Texans fought for the Confederacy. Some of them were well-known Texas Rangers, such as John Ford, who became a colonel in the Second Texas Cavalry. Rancher Benjamin Terry organized and led the Eighth Texas Cavalry—also known as Terry's Texas Rangers—in battles fought from Texas to Tennessee and Kentucky, where Terry died on December 17, 1861, but most historians agree that none of the rebel units called "rangers" were affiliated with the actual Texas Rangers.[23]

Even with the war in progress, proper Rangers still had bloody work to do in Texas. Juan Cortina's outlaws invaded Zapata County in May 1861, whereupon Governor Edward Clark named Henry McCulloch—a former Ranger and brother of Ben McCulloch—to lead the First Regiment of Texas Mounted Riflemen against bandits, hostile Indians, army deserters, and draft dodgers. Governor Pendleton Murrah, elected in November 1863, defied orders that all remaining Texas Rangers and militiamen must join the Confederate army, but superior force compelled his agreement in spring 1864. Murrah then authorized creation of a "Frontier Organization" to replace the missing Rangers and continue their defense of Texas residents.

The Civil War formally ended in Union victory on April 9, 1865, but the last battle occurred on May 13, when "Rip" Ford's cavalry defeated a small Union force at the Battle of Palmito Ranch, in Cameron County, Texas. As usual, Rangers had the last word. No casualty lists exist for Texas Rangers lost during the Civil War, but one famous victim of the conflict was Captain Ben McCulloch, killed in the Battle of Pea Ridge, Arkansas, on March 7–8, 1862.

RECONSTRUCTION AND REUNION

The defeated Southern states were occupied by Union troops and ruled by military governors (except for Tennessee) while new state constitutions were approved, outlawing slavery and granting former slaves the right to vote. Texas plunged into virtual anarchy, haunted by outlaw gangs and violent racist groups such as the Ku Klux Klan, Knights of the White Camellia, and Knights of the Rising Sun. Authorities reported 1,038 murders between April 1865 and June 1868, with 838 victims identified as ex-slaves. General Philip Sheridan, commanding occupation troops in the Lone Star State, said, "If I owned Texas and Hell, I would rent Texas and live in Hell."[24]

President Ulysses Grant approved Texas's readmission to the Union on March 30, 1870. Governor Edmund Davis soon organized 14 companies of Texas Rangers and 41 local groups of "Minute Men" to suppress violent crime. In July the U.S. War Department banned Rangers from Indian-fighting, whereupon Davis ceded control of his Rangers to General Joseph Reynolds and created a new State Police force. While Ranger historian Robert Utley describes the State Police as "hated," they performed well, arresting 4,580 felons (including 829 murderers) between July 1870 and December 1871. Many other known criminals fled the state to avoid arrest.[25]

Despite its readmission to the Union, Texas still had troubled times ahead. Confederate veteran Richard Coke challenged Edmund Davis for the governor's office in December 1873, defeating Davis by a margin of 85,549 votes to 42,633.[26] Davis challenged those results, claiming fraud, but President Grant twice refused calls for troops to keep him in office. Without the State Police, which had dissolved on April 22, 1873, Texas faced the threat of new crime waves to come.

The Late 19th Century

Presidio County, Texas

Outlaws respect no borders. During 1877–1881 a gang led by Henry McCarty—alias Henry Antrim, William Bonney, and "Billy the Kid"—terrorized New Mexico Territory, on the northeast border of Texas. They also crossed the line at will, as in June 1880, when five of McCarty's bandits appeared in Presidio County, on the Rio Grande. Led by Jesse Evans, a prison escapee wanted for murder in New Mexico, they raided Fort Stockton, then rode off in search of more loot.

Fort Stockton's Judge G.M. Frazer telegraphed Company D of the Texas Rangers for help on June 25. Captain Daniel Roberts sent Sergeant E.A. Sieker and eight privates to pursue the gang. They overtook the bandits on July 3, in the Davis Mountains, and engaged in a cross-country chase. Four Rangers with the fastest horses closed the gap, but the outlaws found cover in a gully rimmed by boulders and opened fire with rifles.

Two bullets struck Ranger D.T. Carson's horse, while a third passed through his hat, but Carson returned the fire, wounding gunman George Davis. Sergeant Sieker also fired, killing Davis on the spot. A shot fired by one of the outlaws struck Ranger George "Red" Bingham in the chest, ending his life. Under a hail of Ranger fire, fugitives Evans, John Gross, and two of George Davis's brothers surrendered. The Rangers buried Private Bingham and George Davis together, 18 miles north of the Rio Grande.

Justice was haphazard in 19th-century Texas. Jurors convicted defendants Evans and Gross of Private Bingham's murder and sentenced them to long terms at Huntsville's state prison. The surviving Davis brothers posted bail and were never tried. Jesse Evans escaped from prison on May 23, 1882, and vanished from public records forever. Grateful citizens of Presidio County raised $1,100 as a reward for the surviving Rangers. Back in New Mexico, meanwhile, Sheriff Pat Garrett reportedly shot and killed Billy the Kid on July 14, 1881. Stories persist to this day that McCarty faked his own death and lived on as "John Miller" until 1937. The results of DNA tests performed on Miller's remains in 2005 are still unpublished, ensnared in lawsuits filed by members of his family.

Sheriff Pat Garrett *(foreground)* brings Billy the Kid and his gang to jail. Garrett later shot and killed Billy the Kid in 1881. *(Bettmann/Corbis)*

SUTTON–TAYLOR FEUD

The longest and bloodiest feud in Texas history began soon after the Civil War, in DeWitt County. Josiah Taylor, a transplanted Virginian, led a lawless family of racist ex-Confederates, whose crimes included the murders of four Union soldiers during 1866–1867. Rival William Sutton was a deputy sheriff who pursued local horse thieves in March 1868, killing Charley Taylor and accomplice James Sharp. Nine months later, Buck Taylor and friend Dick Chisholm confronted Sutton in Clinton, and Sutton killed them both. Texas State Police supported Sutton as the feud expanded, laying an ambush that killed Hays Taylor in August 1869. A year later, Sutton arrested two Taylor in-laws, gunning them down in front of witnesses. That incident prompted dismissal of State Police Captain Jack Helm, but Helm retained his post as DeWitt County's sheriff.

The death toll mounted with Pitkin Taylor's murder in summer 1872. The Taylors ambushed Sutton twice in 1872–1873, killing two of his cohorts but failing to slay their main target. Jim Taylor and John Wesley Hardin killed Jack Helm in July

FRONTIER FEUDS

In January 1874 Texas lawmakers created a new Frontier Battalion, consisting of five companies with 75 Texas Rangers in each. Five months later, Governor Richard Coke named Major John B. Jones as the battalion's commander. A native of South Carolina whose family moved to Texas when he was four years old, Jones joined Terry's Texas Rangers as a private, when the Civil War began in 1861, then transferred to the Fifteenth Texas Infantry as a captain. By war's end, according to Ranger historian Wilburn King, Jones "had made an excellent record as a man of superior business tact and judgment, and on the battlefield his coolness, quickness of judgment, breadth of comprehension, soldierly skill, and management had marked him as one to trust in time of difficulty."[1]

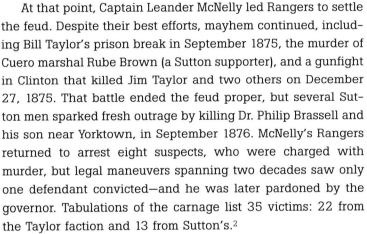

1873, followed by a written truce that lasted five months, until Taylor sympathizer Wiley Pridgen was murdered at Thomaston. Sutton left DeWitt County, but Taylor gunmen found him at Indianola in March 1874. Three months later, Suttonites lynched three Taylor loyalists in Clinton on false charges of rustling cattle.

At that point, Captain Leander McNelly led Rangers to settle the feud. Despite their best efforts, mayhem continued, including Bill Taylor's prison break in September 1875, the murder of Cuero marshal Rube Brown (a Sutton supporter), and a gunfight in Clinton that killed Jim Taylor and two others on December 27, 1875. That battle ended the feud proper, but several Sutton men sparked fresh outrage by killing Dr. Philip Brassell and his son near Yorktown, in September 1876. McNelly's Rangers returned to arrest eight suspects, who were charged with murder, but legal maneuvers spanning two decades saw only one defendant convicted—and he was later pardoned by the governor. Tabulations of the carnage list 35 victims: 22 from the Taylor faction and 13 from Sutton's.[2]

Texas needed such men in the aftermath of Reconstruction, as Indian raids and depredation by outlaws continued. On July 12, 1874, Jones led a company of 40 Rangers against a mixed war party of 125 Apaches, Comanches, and Kiowa at Lost Valley, in Young County. In its first six months of operation, the Frontier Battalion engaged in 14 skirmishes with Indian raiders. Over the next six months, only six fights were recorded, with another six between May 1875 and Major Jones's death in July 1881. Battalion records list 37 hostile Indians killed, versus two Rangers slain and six wounded.[3]

Civil unrest on other fronts also kept the Rangers busy. In June 1874, while Rangers tried to end the bloody Sutton-Taylor Feud in Clinton and DeWitt Counties, widespread cattle rustling sparked the "Hoodoo War" (one of a number of feuds that developed over the stealing and killing of cattle) in Mason County. Sheriff John Clark arrested nine alleged rustlers, four of whom escaped before a mob of 40 men removed the rest from jail and lynched them in February 1875. Captain Daniel Roberts pursued the mob with a party of Rangers but made no arrests. Another lynching, of suspect Tim Williamson, followed in May 1875, and violence escalated when a friend of Williamson—ex-Ranger Scott Cooley—swore revenge against his killers.

Cooley and his followers blamed German immigrants in Mason County for Williamson's death, and their retaliation claimed at least a dozen lives by autumn 1876. In August 1875 Governor Coke sent Major Jones and 30 Rangers to quell the bloodshed. Still, violence continued, with varied reports confusing events and names of the victims. Jones searched for ex-Ranger Cooley in vain, dismissing some of his own men who were friends of Cooley and had warned him of impending raids. Several suspects were arrested, but in most cases the charges were dismissed. No defendant on either side was ever convicted of murder, but uneasy peace returned to Mason County in the winter of 1876–1877. On January 21, 1877, arsonists burned the county courthouse, destroying all legal records pertaining to the feud.[4]

In the spring of 1875 Captain Leander McNelly (1844–1877) assumed command of a new Ranger company patrolling the Nueces Strip, between the Nueces and Rio Grande rivers. They pursued cross-border raiders led by Juan Cortina—now a general in the Mexican army—but stormed the wrong ranch and missed their quarry. Next, McNelly led 30 Rangers across the border into Mexico, where they seized 75 stolen cattle, then found themselves surrounded by Mexican troops and bandits. Although outgunned, and facing reprimands from U.S. diplomats for the illegal border crossing, McNelly refused to leave Mexico without the Texas cattle. Mexican authorities agreed, while refusing to surrender suspected rustlers, and McNelly went home to be relieved of duty, replaced by Captain Jesse Hall.[5]

The year 1877 found Texas Rangers immersed in El Paso County's "Salt War" (where opposing factions fought for control of valuable salt beds) and the deadly Horrell–Higgins Feud, in Lampasas County. That conflict involved two neighboring families that seemed friendly prior to Reconstruction, later falling out when the five Horrell brothers began stealing cattle. State Police officers sought to arrest them in 1873, spark-

SALT WARS

The "salt war" began as a late-1860s political contest for control of salt deposits near Guadalupe Creek, 100 miles east of El Paso. The first violence occurred in December 1870, with the murder of Judge Gaylord Clarke. Competition resumed in 1872, between Anglo officials and Hispanics led by Louis Cardis. Judge Charles Howard filed a claim on the salt lakes, enraging Hispanics who considered them public property. Rioters held Howard hostage for three days in September 1877, until he renounced his claim and fled to New Mexico, but Howard returned a month later and killed Cardis in El Paso. Lieutenant John Tays led a Ranger detachment to arrest Howard and arraign him on murder charges.

In December 1877 16 wagons left El Paso for the salt lakes. Howard filed lawsuits against the trespassers, sparking another riot in San Elizario—then the seat of El Paso County—that left two men dead, while rioters besieged the Rangers and Howard. Federal troops were dispatched but refused to enter San Elizario. On December 14 the Rangers surrendered their weapons and were allowed to leave town—the only such incident in Texas history. Three days later, a Mexican firing squad executed Howard and companion John Atkinson, while rioters looted San Elizario. U.S. troops and local vigilantes finally advanced, killing four men and wounding several more, while most of the rebels escaped into Mexico. Several suspects were indicted, but none were ever captured or convicted. As a result of the salt war, U.S. troops manned nearby Fort Bliss, San Elizario lost its status as county seat to El Paso, and a new railroad bypassed the town in 1883, causing its population and influence to decline.

ing a battle that left four policemen dead and Mart Horrell in custody, badly wounded. Horrell's brothers later broke him out of jail and fled to New Mexico, where they continued rustling on both sides of the border.

New Mexico authorities drove the Horrells back into Texas late in 1874, and while they finally faced trial for murder, all were acquitted.

Trouble continued through 1875–1876, as John Higgins accused the Horrells of stealing his livestock. In January 1877, Higgins killed Merritt Horrell in a Lampasas saloon, and various battles followed, claiming at least 17 lives. Major Jones led a Ranger detachment into the war zone and negotiated a treaty of sorts between the combatants on July 30, 1877. Both sides agreed to consider the feud "a by gone thing," but the Horrells continued their lives of crime. In 1878, brothers Mart and Tom were accused of robbery and murder in Bosque County, hunted down and executed by a vigilante gang. Sam Horrell, sole survivor of the family, left Texas for Oregon in 1882.[6]

FAST GUNS

Post-Civil War Texas produced some of the Wild West's most notorious gunmen, including John King Fisher (1854–1884), John Wesley Hardin (1853–1895), and Sam Bass (1851–1878). Texas Rangers hunted each in turn, with varying results.

Fisher was a Collin County native, first charged with horse theft at age 15. The horse's owner declined to press charges, but later a burglary at Goliad sent Fisher to prison. Pardoned four months later, he moved to Dimmit County, in the Nueces Strip, and established a ranch that served as a cover for wholesale cattle rustling. Known for gaudy outfits and twin silver-plated, pearl-handled revolvers, Fisher was notoriously arrogant, posting a highway near his ranch with a sign reading: "This is King Fisher's road. Take the other." Various published accounts credit Fisher with five to 13 homicides, "not counting Mexicans."[7]

Ranger Captains Leander McNelly and Jesse Hall arrested Fisher several times, and while jurors refused to convict him, legal problems wore Fisher down over time. He bought a new ranch in 1876, became a deputy sheriff in 1883, and was appointed as Uvalde County's acting sheriff when his predecessor was convicted of bribery. Fisher campaigned for election to a full term in 1884 but never made it. On March 11 he and a friend, notorious gunman Ben Thompson, quarreled with the owner of a theater in San Antonio, provoking a gunfight that left them both dead.

John Wesley Hardin may have been America's deadliest gunfighter. Most accounts claim that he killed 40 men or more, though one trims Hardin's tally to 11. A minister's son who went bad, Hardin stabbed his first victim—a rare survivor—at age 11, then shot and killed an unarmed former slave at age 15. His other victims included three lawmen and four Union soldiers, slain while trying to arrest Hardin for

John Wesley Hardin was the most notorious killer and quick-draw gunman in Texas in the late 1800s. (*Bettmann/Corbis*)

various crimes.[8] Some Texans of the violent Reconstruction era viewed Hardin as a hero, though today he would probably rank as a serial killer.

Texas Rangers began tracking Hardin in May 1874, after he killed Deputy Sheriff Charles Webb in Comanche County. He eluded them until August 23, 1877, when Rangers John Armstrong and Jack Duncan found Hardin and three other gunmen on a train at Pensacola, Florida. Single-handed, Armstrong clubbed Hardin unconscious, killed companion Jim Mann (who put a bullet hole in Armstrong's hat), and disarmed the other shooters. Texas jurors convicted Hardin of Webb's murder in September 1878, and he served 16 years of a 25-year sentence. Hardin became a lawyer after his release from prison in 1894, but his history of violence followed him. Constable John Selman killed Hardin in an El Paso barroom on August 19, 1895. Some called it murder, but Selman faced no charges. He died in a shootout with fellow lawman George Scarborough on April 5, 1896.

Sam Bass was born in Indiana, orphaned at age 13, and sent to live with an uncle. He fled that home in 1869 and reached Texas the following year, soon discovering that he disliked the hard work of an honest cowboy's life. Gambling and rustling seemed more attractive occupations, expanded to include armed robbery with several friends by 1877. The Bass gang ranged as far afield as Nebraska, where they scored $61,000 in their first train robbery. In the spring of 1878 the team robbed four trains within 25 miles of Dallas, thus drawing attention from the Texas Rangers.

The outlaw trail ended for Bass and his cohorts at Round Rock, Texas, where they planned to rob a bank on July 20, 1878. With three companions, Bass rode into town a day early, unaware that gang member Jim Murphy had betrayed him to the Rangers, hoping to receive a shorter prison sentence for himself. On July 19, when Bass, Seaborn Barnes, and Frank Johnson entered a shop next door to Round Rock's bank, Deputy Sheriffs Ellis Grimes and Morris Moore sought to arrest them. The bandits shot both lawmen, killing Grimes, and then tried to flee on horseback. Ranger Dick Ware killed Barnes in the street, while Ranger George Harrell shot Bass from his saddle. Jackson, uninjured, helped Bass escape, but a posse found Bass outside town the next morning, weak from loss of blood. He died on July 21, still refusing to speak with police.

LAW AND ORDER, RANGER STYLE

In the last two decades of the 19th century, Texas Rangers handled a wide range of duties. While Texas's Indian wars officially ended with the surrender of Chief Quannah Parker in June 1875, trouble resumed in April 1877, when federal authorities ordered Apaches removed to Arizona. War chiefs Victorio, Loco, and Poinsenay fled to Mexico, staging cross-border raids in Texas and New Mexico over the next three years.

Ranger Lieutenant George Baylor's Company C pursued Victorio without success during that period, illegally crossing the Mexican border on a fruitless search in September 1880. Mexican troops killed Victorio and most of his warriors a month later, while Baylor was promoted to captain in charge of Ranger Company A. In 1881, after a few surviving raiders robbed a stagecoach near Diablo Mountain, Baylor struck their camp and ended the final Apache resistance.

That victory earned Baylor another promotion in 1882, to major in charge of several Ranger companies. A year later, his men were deployed to quell violence between free-range cattlemen and settlers who fenced their ranches. A "fence war" erupted in summer 1883, with countless fences cut by night-prowling gangs that called themselves "Blue Devils," "Javelinas," and "Owls." Sometimes, the raiders set fire to pastures and barns. At least three men were dead, and property damage was estimated at $20 million, when Governor John Ireland convened a special legislative session to address the problem in October 1873. Three months later, a new law imposed five-year prison terms for fence cutting and pasture burning, while farmers who had built fences on public land or roads were ordered to remove them or face misdemeanor prosecution.[9] Trouble still flared from time to time, as in Navarro County during 1888, and Rangers investigated occasional fence-cutting cases into the 1890s.

Revolution to the south, in Mexico, continued to affect Texas, in large part thanks to journalist Catarino Garza Rodriguez (1859–1895). Born in Matamoros but a resident of Brownsville, Texas, from age 21, Garza publicized human-rights violations by the Mexican government and Anglo officials alike. In 1888 he criticized ex-Ranger Victor Sebree for killing robbery suspect Abraham Reséndez and was charged with libel. Ranger Captain John Hughes arrested Garza and took him to Rio

Grande City, where Sebree shot and wounded Garza. That provoked a riot, as 200 Garza supporters sought to lynch Sebree, forcing him to flee the city (though he did not lose his job as a U.S. Customs inspector). Garza moved to South America in 1893, and reportedly died in March 1895, while leading a raid on a jail in present-day Panama.

Each day brought some new challenge to the Rangers. During 1894–1895 they scouted 173,381 miles of Texas frontier, arrested 676 suspects, returned 2,856 head of stolen livestock to the rightful owners, assisted local authorities 162 times, and guarded jails on 13 occasions.[10]

In February 1896, El Paso authorities banned a scheduled prizefight between heavyweight champion Robert Fitzsimmons and challenger Peter Maher. Boxing fans threatened mob violence, whereupon Ranger Captain William McDonald arrived to prevent disorder. When El Paso's mayor asked McDonald if he was alone, McDonald replied, "Ain't I enough? There's only one prizefight!" That comment inspired the famous slogan: "One riot, one Ranger."[11] Controversial judge Roy Bean solved the problem by staging the fight on a sandbar in the Rio Grande, where Texas lawmen had no jurisdiction.

At the close of the 19th century, Rangers found themselves embroiled in the Laredo "smallpox riot," sparked by events in October 1898. The trouble began on October 4, when a Mexican child died from smallpox. Laredo physicians had more than 100 cases on file by January 1899, when state authorities ordered wholesale vaccinations, quarantines, and fumigation of Hispanic barrios. In March, some angry residents began resisting vaccination. Rangers arrived on March 19, to ensure compliance, but they met a furious crowd of Mexican Americans. Violence erupted on March 20, when a local marshal was wounded by gunshots. Rangers exchanged fire with a mob of 100 rioters, leaving one man dead and 13 wounded. Federal troops arrived to crush the riot on March 22, and smallpox deaths continued into April. Laredo's quarantine was lifted on May 1, 1899.[12]

A hurricane struck Galveston, Texas, on September 8, 1900, killing at least 6,000 people (some reports claim 12,000 dead), destroying 2,636 homes, and causing property damage estimated at $20 million to $30 million ($529 million to $794 million today). Texas Rangers helped in rescue efforts and suppression of looting after the storm, even as political forces undermined their authority by abolishing the Frontier Battalion.[13]

Galveston's tragedy was also the Frontier Battalion's last hurrah. Fifteen weeks earlier—on May 26, 1900—a state supreme court ruling held that only commissioned Ranger officers (those holding ranks of lieutenant or higher) were entitled to make arrests. The force was not disbanded, as some authors claim, but it was relegated to a sideline role, viewed by many as a relic of the bygone Wild West era. Still, as historian Walter Webb granted, the Rangers had made Texas "a fairly safe place in which to live."[14]

Lawless Years

Cameron County, Texas

Brothers Alfredo and Ramón de la Cerda were notorious cattle rustlers, like their father before them. A Brownsville policeman killed the family's patriarch in 1900, but the brothers kept rustling, staging repeated raids against the 825,000-acre King Ranch that sprawled over parts of four counties in southern Texas. In 1901 three Rangers—Sergeant A.Y. Baker, with Privates Emmett Robuck and Harry Wallis—were patrolling the King Ranch when they found Ramón de la Cerda changing the brand on a steer. As they told the story, Cerda fired at the Rangers, killing Baker's horse, and then Baker fired in self-defense, killing Cerda.

A coroner's inquest ruled the slaying justified, but Cerda's relatives exhumed his corpse six days later, for an independent autopsy. That report claimed that Cerda was beaten, bound, and dragged behind a horse before he died. The Rangers were charged with murder, released on $10,000 bond, but then cleared at a second inquest.[1] That judgment only increased the rage of Cerda's relatives.

On the night of September 9, 1902, Sergeant Baker and Private Robuck were approaching the Ranger camp at Brownsville with Private Jesse Miller when gunmen fired at them from ambush. A shotgun blast killed Robuck, while rifle bullets killed one of the Rangers' horses and wounded Baker in the leg. The shooters escaped, but Ranger Captain John Brooks soon arrested Alfredo de la Cerda and four other suspects. Prosecution witness Heroulano Berbier told authorities that Alfredo had threatened to kill Baker or pay $1,000 to anyone who did, but unknown gunmen murdered Berbier before he could testify under oath.

Authorities released Alfredo on bail, but he never stood trial. On October 3, 1902, Sergeant Baker shot Cerda with a rifle, through the window of a Brownsville store. Baker claimed that Cerda had drawn a pistol, but other witnesses said Cerda was unarmed and trying on gloves when he died. Thomas Fernandez described Baker "stalking [Cerda] like a wild animal." Judge Stanley Welch praised Baker "for having performed a service which the local officers were unable to do," but a grand jury charged Baker with murder. Jurors acquitted Baker on October 13, after deliberating for 20 minutes. Baker later served as a U.S. Customs inspector and as sheriff of Hidalgo County.[2]

RANGERS REBORN

On July 8, 1901, the Texas state legislature authorized four new Ranger companies of "no more than 20 men each," empowered to "protect the frontier against marauding or thieving parties and for the suppression of lawlessness and crime throughout the state."[3] Captains would be appointed by the governor, with each authorized to choose his own Rangers. Those selected would provide their own horses and weapons, and wear their own clothes. The state did not even provide standard badges.

While Indian raiding had ceased in Texas, there was no shortage of crime for Rangers to investigate. The state's first significant oil strike had occurred in January 1901, at Spindletop in Jefferson County, and others soon followed. "Boomtowns" sprang up overnight around the sites of oil discoveries, swarming with fortune hunters and those who preyed on them: claim jumpers and bandits, saloon keepers, gamblers, and prostitutes. Communities like Beaumont, Breckenridge, Bridgetown, Burkburnett, Cisco, Desdemona, Eastland, Gladewater, Kilgore, and Odessa existed in near-chaos until small detachments of Rangers arrived to suppress lawlessness.

Brownsville produced more trouble in 1906, between white residents and black soldiers of the 25th Infantry at nearby Fort Brown. Racist discrimination caused tension, and authorities blamed soldiers for a shooting that killed one white man and wounded two on August

Texas Rangers stand for a photograph after a recent raid on the town of Kilgore, the small Texas town that mushroomed overnight with an oil boom. The raid netted 300 undesirable characters who had brought violence and lawlessness to the town. *(Bettmann/Corbis)*

13. Ranger Captain William McDonald blamed 12 soldiers for the shooting, but a grand jury refused to indict them. President Theodore Roosevelt dishonorably discharged all 167 black soldiers in November, for an alleged "conspiracy of silence." In 1972, President Richard Nixon awarded honorable discharges to all 167 soldiers. The sole survivor received a $25,000 pension.

Five Rangers died violently in the first decade of the 20th century, but the rest persevered.[4] Their attitude was summarized by Captain William McDonald in his 1909 biography and by his epitaph in 1918:

"No man in the wrong can stand up against a fellow that's in the right and keeps on a-comin.'"[5]

REVOLUTION!

In 1910 the harsh policies of President Porfirio Diaz sparked revolution among Mexico's peasants and working class. Successor Francisco Madero tried to institute reforms during 1911–1913, but General Vitoriano Huerta deposed Madero with covert support from U.S. ambassador Henry Lane Wilson and imposed a military dictatorship. President Woodrow Wilson fired Lane and refused to recognize Huerta's regime, while domestic opposition to Huerta plunged Mexico into civil war. Huerta fled to Spain in 1914, leaving various rivals battling for control of Mexico until 1920.

The violence spilled over into Texas, with guerrillas and nonpolitical bandits raiding towns and ranches along the border. In January 1915, Mexican refugees and radicals hatched the "Plan of San Diego," drafting the blueprint for a "Liberating Army of Races and Peoples" that would "free" the states of Arizona, California, Colorado, New Mexico, and Texas from U.S. control, to form an independent nation or reunite with Mexico, as the inhabitants preferred. The revolution was scheduled to begin on February 20, but authorities found a copy of the plan on January 24, sparking panic among whites.

Published accounts disagree on what happened next. Author Benjamin Johnson claims that a flurry of raids carried out by plotters and guerrillas serving under Mexican revolutionary Francisco "Pancho" Villa killed more than 500 Anglo Texans within a matter of weeks.[6] The Texas State Historical Association disagrees, stating that "[f]atalities directly linked to the raids were surprisingly small; between July 1915 and July 1916 some 30 raids into Texas produced only 21 American deaths, both civilian and military. More destructive and disruptive was the near race war that ensued in the wake of the plan as relations between the whites and the Mexicans and Mexican Americans deteriorated in 1915–1916. Federal reports indicated that more than 300 Mexicans or Mexican Americans were summarily executed in South Texas in the atmosphere generated by the plan."[7]

Texas Rangers played a part in that bloodshed. Governor Oscar Colquitt had reduced the Rangers to a force of 13 men in 1911, but soon regretted his decision, instructing Captain John Hughes that "you and your men are to keep Mexican raiders off of Texas territory if possible, and if they invade the State let them understand they do so at the risk of their lives." Hundreds of "special" Rangers were recruited without careful screening, and the results were predictable. Historians report that "[t]he regular rangers, along with hundreds of special rangers appointed by Texas governors, killed approximately 5,000 Hispanics between 1914 and 1919, a source of scandal and embarrassment."[8] The most notorious such incident, dubbed the Porvenir Massacre, where Rangers tortured and murdered innocent Mexicans, occurred in January 1918.

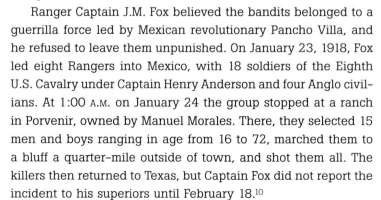

THE PORVENIR MASSACRE

On December 25, 1917, a gang of 45 Mexican bandits raided Lucas Brite's ranch and store in Presidio County, Texas, killing three persons and looting the store. U.S. cavalry troops pursued the raiders into Mexico, killing 10 near Pilares, Chihuahua, and recovering some of the loot. The rest of the gang escaped.[9]

Ranger Captain J.M. Fox believed the bandits belonged to a guerrilla force led by Mexican revolutionary Pancho Villa, and he refused to leave them unpunished. On January 23, 1918, Fox led eight Rangers into Mexico, with 18 soldiers of the Eighth U.S. Cavalry under Captain Henry Anderson and four Anglo civilians. At 1:00 A.M. on January 24 the group stopped at a ranch in Porvenir, owned by Manuel Morales. There, they selected 15 men and boys ranging in age from 16 to 72, marched them to a bluff a quarter-mile outside of town, and shot them all. The killers then returned to Texas, but Captain Fox did not report the incident to his superiors until February 18.[10]

LOYALTY RANGERS

The outbreak of World War I in 1914, with resultant fears of foreign spies and saboteurs, increased tension along the Rio Grande. In January 1917 state lawmakers passed the Hobby Loyalty Act, creating a special "Loyalty Ranger Force" with three agents in each Texas county. Loyalty Rangers were a state equivalent of the U.S. Secret Service, authorized to work with federal and local law enforcement agencies to keep track of Mexican revolutionaries and any other foreign threats against the Lone Star State.

The Mexican threat seemed real in those days, following exposure of a telegram written by German Foreign Secretary Arthur Zimmermann and sent by German ambassador Johann von Bernstorff to his counterpart in Mexico on January 19, 1917. Aside from plans for unrestricted

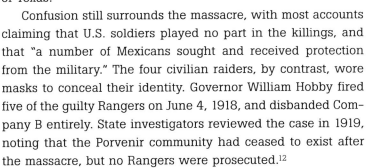

In his report, Fox claimed that those killed had fired on the Rangers and soldiers without provocation. When arrested and disarmed, Fox said, the suspects were found in possession of shoes, soap, and pocket knives stolen from Lucas Brite's store. Fox also claimed that one of those slain had threatened a raid against "Texas Gringos" nine months before the Brite Ranch raid. Further investigation proved that all of those killed at Porvenir were actually Mexican–American residents of Texas.[11]

Confusion still surrounds the massacre, with most accounts claiming that U.S. soldiers played no part in the killings, and that "a number of Mexicans sought and received protection from the military." The four civilian raiders, by contrast, wore masks to conceal their identity. Governor William Hobby fired five of the guilty Rangers on June 4, 1918, and disbanded Company B entirely. State investigators reviewed the case in 1919, noting that the Porvenir community had ceased to exist after the massacre, but no Rangers were prosecuted.[12]

submarine warfare against shipping in the Atlantic Ocean, the telegram proposed "an alliance on the following basis with Mexico: That we shall make war together and make peace together. We shall give generous financial support, and an understanding on our part that Mexico is to reconquer the lost territory in New Mexico, Texas, and Arizona."[13]

Mexican president Venustiano Carranza considered the proposal, and while he rejected it as impractical, the very suggestion sparked new fears and anger in Texas. Police and vigilante violence against Hispanics increased, with Texas Rangers in the thick of it. After the United States entered World War I in April 1917, Governor James Ferguson appointed 400 more Special Rangers to patrol the border and guard against subversion. By the war's end, in November 1918, hundreds—or thousands—were dead across Texas, with animosity between Anglos and Hispanics at its highest point since the Mexican War.

In January 1919, Representative José Canales of Brownsville called for an investigation of Ranger activities. While no conclusive casualty figures were compiled, state legislators determined that Rangers had slain at least 300 persons—and perhaps as many as 5,000—between 1910 and 1918. Brutality was commonplace. Lawmakers pledged to purge the force of vigilantes and ensure professionalism by hiring only "men of high moral character." To that end, on March 13, 1919, new legislation disbanded the Special Rangers and reduced the regular force to four companies of 15 men each. A headquarters company, based in Austin, was also established with six Rangers serving under a senior captain.[14]

Ironically, that change came just as Texas—and America at large—faced another historic crime wave.

PROHIBITION

The American temperance movement, opposing all forms of alcoholic beverages, began 10 years before Texas won independence from Mexico. Twenty-three states banned booze in all forms between 1912 and 1917, when Congress passed the Eighteenth Amendment to the U.S. Constitution, outlawing most alcoholic drinks nationwide. Ratified in 36 states by January 16, 1919, the amendment and a federal law enforcing it—the Volstead Act—took effect one year later.[15] Texas beat the deadline by going "dry" in May 1918.

Much of the enforcement work for Prohibition fell to state and local police. Congress launched its war on booze with only 1,520 federal agents in 1920, increased to a mere 2,836—56 per state—by 1930. Most of those were stationed in large cities and along the Canadian border, and many, struggling with paychecks of $35 to $50 per week, gladly accepted bribes to ignore liquor shipments.[16] In Texas, Rangers worked with the outnumbered feds and local officers to catch smugglers crossing the Rio Grande or landing alcoholic cargo from the Gulf of Mexico, to close outlawed saloons, and dismantle illegal distilleries.

Prohibition enforcement was dangerous business. Nationwide, between 1920 and 1932, 512 federal agents and an uncertain number of local officers were slain by bootleggers, while lawmen killed at least 2,089 suspects. Texas feds were relatively lucky, losing only four men killed, and while historian Mike Cox reports that "shoot-outs between Rangers and smugglers were not infrequent," only one Ranger died in combat with bootleggers. Ranger Timothy Willard was shot while raiding a moonshine still with federal agents on April 19, 1928, but lived long enough to name his killer—a 70-year-old man who received a 99-year prison term for murder.[17]

The Twenty-first Amendment to the Constitution repealed Prohibition in December 1933, but much of Texas remained "dry" long after alcohol was legalized nationwide. As of 2009, liquor sales still were banned or restricted in 48 of the state's 254 counties.[18]

BLACK GOLD

The challenges of oil boomtowns persisted through the 1920s and beyond, aggravating the problem of Prohibition enforcement as bootleggers, gamblers, and prostitutes flocked to wide-open settlements. Time after time, as local officers failed to control their communities, Rangers were dispatched to suppress rampant crime.

One case in point was Mexia, in Limestone County, which expanded from 3,000 residents in October 1921 to 30,000 in January 1922. On January 6, Governor Pat Neff sent Rangers to close illegal saloons, casinos, and dance halls that were little more than brothels. Despite their best efforts, the crime wave continued until Neff sent troops and declared martial law on January 13.[19]

Five years later, in April 1927, Governor Dan Moody sent two Ranger captains and eight privates to clean up the oil town of Borger, in Hutchinson County. As described in the state adjutant general's report: "A thorough-going clean-up was put underway. The liquor traffic was broken up, many stills being seized and destroyed, and several thousand gallons of whiskey being captured and poured out. Two hundred and three gambling slot machines were seized and destroyed ... and in a period of twenty-four hours ... no less than 1,200 prostitutes left the town of Borger."[20]

Crime was even worse in Eastland County, at Ranger—ironically named for a 19th-century Texas Ranger camp. Modern Rangers arrived to find 16,000 scofflaws running rampant, and the local jail soon overflowed. Never deterred by such small problems, the Rangers shackled surplus criminals to phone poles, pending trial.[21]

Rangers received unwelcome aid in law enforcement from the 1920s Ku Klux Klan, revived with some 400,000 Texas members and a list of enemies including African Americans, Hispanics, Jews, Roman Catholics, most immigrants, and anyone who deviated from the Klan's view of "morality." In 1922 alone, Klansmen whipped, killed, or tarred-and-feathered more than 500 victims. Violence declined the following year, when Rangers began arresting violent Klansmen—including Taylor's police chief.[22]

DEPRESSION AND DECLINE

Texas suffered as much from the Great Depression of 1929–1941 as any other state, and Rangers were not immune. Most remembered Governor James "Pa" Ferguson for the bribery charges that prompted his resignation in 1917, and they had not been pleased when his wife—Miriam "Ma" Ferguson—served as governor in 1925–1927. Her administration was corrupt, including an average 100 pardons for convicted felons each month, and Rangers supported incumbent Ross Sterling when Ma sought a second term in 1932. Her victory was a disaster for the Texas Rangers.[23]

Forty Rangers resigned in January 1933, while Ferguson fired the remaining 44 for opposing her re-election. State lawmakers slashed Ranger salaries and travel budgets, eliminated longevity pay, and lim-

Miriam "Ma" Ferguson was the first female governor of Texas. James "Pa" Ferguson, her husband, was the governor of Texas from 1915 to 1917, when he was impeached and convicted on several charges. The ruling declared that he could no longer hold office in Texas, but he ran his wife's campaigns; she was elected governor of Texas in 1925 and 1933. *(Bettmann/Corbis)*

ited the Rangers to a total of 32 men. Governor Ferguson appointed those, described by historian Steve Schuster as "a contemptible lot." Within a year, one new Ranger was convicted of murder, and a captain was jailed on charges of theft and embezzlement, and others from Company D established their own illegal casino to replace one they had closed. Worse yet, Ferguson appointed 2,344 "Special Rangers" from the ranks of her political supporters. The *Austin American* observed that "about all the requirements a person needed...to be a Special Ranger was to be a human being."[24]

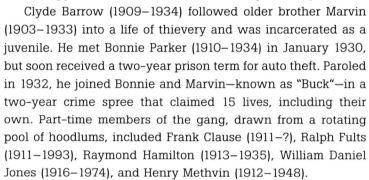

BONNIE AND CLYDE

Members of the 1930s Barrow gang bore little resemblance to the romantic characters portrayed by Hollywood in the 1967 film *Bonnie and Clyde*. They were small-time bandits and brutal killers whose 12 murder victims included nine lawmen. Unlike other gangs of the era, they rarely robbed banks and never bagged more than $1,500 from a single holdup.

Clyde Barrow (1909–1934) followed older brother Marvin (1903–1933) into a life of thievery and was incarcerated as a juvenile. He met Bonnie Parker (1910–1934) in January 1930, but soon received a two-year prison term for auto theft. Paroled in 1932, he joined Bonnie and Marvin—known as "Buck"—in a two-year crime spree that claimed 15 lives, including their own. Part-time members of the gang, drawn from a rotating pool of hoodlums, included Frank Clause (1911–?), Ralph Fults (1911–1993), Raymond Hamilton (1913–1935), William Daniel Jones (1916–1974), and Henry Methvin (1912–1948).

Bonnie and Clyde were Texas natives, but they roamed as far north as Minnesota in stolen cars, robbing stores and gas stations, stealing weapons from National Guard armories, fighting pitched battles with police and local vigilantes. Buck

Sadly, the Ranger decline occurred as a new crime wave swamped Texas and America at large with robberies and ransom kidnappings. Notorious Lone Star outlaws included George "Machine Gun" Kelly, the Hamilton brothers, and the deadly team of Clyde Barrow and Bonnie Parker. Outlaws had robbed so many banks by early 1928 that the Texas Bankers Association offered a $5,000 reward for any bandit killed during a holdup. Nothing was offered for those caught alive.[25]

By 1934, corruption in the Ferguson administration was so flagrant that state legislators launched a sweeping investigation. With regard to the Rangers, lawmakers recommended creating a new agency to handle

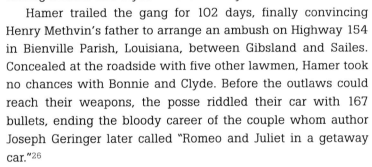

died in an Iowa shootout in July 1933, while Bonnie and Clyde were wounded. Texas Rangers hunted the gang, but relatives in Dallas sheltered the fugitives, and the Rangers had no jurisdiction outside Texas.

That changed in January 1934, when the gang staged a jailbreak at the Eastham prison farm, killing one guard and wounding another as they freed Ray Hamilton, Henry Methvin, and three other convicts. Lee Simmons, head of the Texas Department of Corrections, swore vengeance against the killers. He assigned retired Ranger Captain Frank Hamer (1884–1955) to track the gang as a special investigator, following Bonnie and Clyde wherever they ran.

Hamer trailed the gang for 102 days, finally convincing Henry Methvin's father to arrange an ambush on Highway 154 in Bienville Parish, Louisiana, between Gibsland and Sailes. Concealed at the roadside with five other lawmen, Hamer took no chances with Bonnie and Clyde. Before the outlaws could reach their weapons, the posse riddled their car with 167 bullets, ending the bloody career of the couple whom author Joseph Geringer later called "Romeo and Juliet in a getaway car."[26]

statewide crime prevention and detection. Governor James Allred, elected to replace Ma Ferguson in 1934, launched his new administration by dismissing all the Rangers she had appointed. On August 10, 1935, lawmakers created the Texas Department of Public Safety, supervised by a three-member Public Safety Commission. The fate of the Rangers remained uncertain.

A New Department

Starr County, Texas

In May 1966 a leader for the National Farm Workers' Association, Eugene Nelson, helped Texas migrant workers organize the Independent Workers' Association (IWA), based in Rio Grande City. The union's goal was a minimum wage of $1.25 per hour and "recognition as a bargaining force" in the Rio Grande valley. When planters refused to negotiate, Nelson launched a strike by melon pickers on June 1. Texas Rangers and sheriff's deputies arrested many of the strikers—most of whom were Mexican Americans—and local judges set high bonds to keep union members in jail. In response, the union marched on Austin for meetings with Governor John Connally and other state officials.

Demonstrations failed to win a breakthrough for the IWA, and tension increased as the May 1967 melon harvest approached. Charges of police brutality spawned investigations by the U.S. Commission on Civil Rights, the U.S. Senate Subcommittee on Migratory Labor, and the Texas Council of Churches, revealing that Rangers under Captain Alfred Allee had beaten union members Magdeleno Dimas and Reverend Edgar Krueger on June 1, 1967. A state court blocked further arrests of protesters in July 1967, and union leaders filed a federal lawsuit against Allee's Rangers for violating their civil rights.[1]

Captain Allee retired from the Texas Rangers in 1970, two years before a federal court ruled that Texas statutes banning union picket lines were unconstitutional, also finding that the Rangers had engaged in "a persistent pattern of police misconduct." Allee appealed that verdict to the U.S. Supreme Court, which upheld the lower court's judgment in May 1974.[2]

THE NEW BREED

Times were changing when author Walter Webb's history of the Texas Rangers went to press in 1935. Creation of the new Department of Public Safety (DPS) caused Webb to add an epilogue declaring that the new law amounted to "practical abolition of the [Ranger] force." Webb told his readers: "It is safe to say that as time goes on the functions of the un-uniformed Texas Rangers will gradually slip away."[3]

Most Rangers feared that Webb was correct—but his prediction proved inaccurate. In fact, the DPS included three separate units: the Texas Rangers, the Highway Patrol, and a Headquarters Division equipped with a modern crime laboratory. The Rangers kept their five-company structure—35 men under Senior Captain Tom Hickman—but hiring procedures were changed. Recruits were limited to men between the ages of 30 and 45, who were at least five feet eight inches tall and "perfectly sound" in both body and mind. No education standards were imposed, but applicants had to pass a written test and prove themselves "crack shots." Political appointments were banned, and once hired, each Ranger had to file "intelligent" weekly reports of his activities. All were trained in new techniques of fingerprinting, communications, ballistics testing, and record keeping. Promotions were based solely on seniority and performance.[4]

Despite those improvements and a busy schedule—255 investigations in their first year with the DPS—some Rangers still worried about their agency's future until September 1938, when Colonel Homer Garrison Jr. (1901–1968) took office as the department's director. Garrison entered law enforcement as a 19-year-old sheriff's deputy in Angelina County, became an inspector for the state highway department in 1929, then joined the Highway Patrol at its creation in 1930. In 1935 he helped organize the New Mexico State Police, then was appointed as first assistant director of the Texas DPS in August 1935, graduating to its top post three years later. Under Garrison the Rangers became the state's plainclothes detective force, stationed

Colonel Homer Garrison Jr., director of the Department of Public Safety in Texas from 1938 until his death in 1968, poses for a photograph in 1950. *(Bettmann/Corbis)*

individually in small rural towns and available for special assignments as needed.[5]

WORLD WAR II

One year after Colonel Garrison assumed command of the DPS, German troops invaded Poland and began World War II in Europe. In the Far East, Adolf Hitler's Japanese allies had already invaded China, expanding to threaten territory owned by Britain, France, and the Netherlands. America remained officially neutral until Japanese aircraft attacked Pearl Harbor, Hawaii, in December 1941, but some Texas Rangers were ready to fight from day one.

Soon after the European war began, in September 1939, Captain Frank Hamer and 49 retired Rangers offered their services to King George VI of Britain, as volunteers to defend England against Nazi invaders. The king declined, with thanks, while spokesmen for the U.S. State Department complained of Ranger meddling in international affairs. Later, Hitler's Gestapo (secret police) pursued rumors that Rangers planned to infiltrate Germany. Those stories probably arose from confused descriptions of the U.S. Army Rangers, a combat unit formed in May 1942 whose members did not reach Europe until D-Day, in June 1944.[6]

In 1941 the Rangers expanded to include six companies and a total of 45 men. When the United States entered World War II that December, Rangers added civil defense tasks to their normal list of crime-fighting duties. Some conducted air raid warning drills, while others arrested enemy aliens, guarded strategic dams and factories against sabotage, trained agents of the U.S. Army's Criminal Intelligence Division, or tracked escapees from camps confining prisoners of war (POWs).

Thanks to its vast size and climate, Texas had twice as many POW camps as any other U.S. state. The Geneva Convention required that prisoners be housed in climates similar to those where they were captured, and Pentagon officials seemed to think that Texas resembled North Africa, where thousands of German soldiers surrendered. Official records kept during 1942–1945 list only 21 escapees from 33 POW camps scattered across Texas—most from Hearne and Mexia—but none remained at large for long. Some of the escapes were comical: one fugitive was treed by a bad-tempered bull; another was spotted near Franklin, singing German army marching songs as he hiked along U.S. Highway 79; and three others were caught while trying to reach Europe on a raft—along the Brazos River.[7]

At the war's end, in 1945, General Douglas MacArthur offered Colonel Garrison a job with the U.S. War Department, reorganizing the

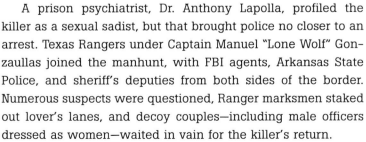

MURDER BY MOONLIGHT

Serial killers have existed throughout history, although the term was not coined until the early 1960s. One of America's most mystifying cases terrorized Texarkana, on the Texas-Arkansas border, during 1946, as an unknown slayer struck repeatedly on nights of the full moon. Dubbed the "Moonlight Murderer" and "Phantom Killer," the stalker was never brought to justice.

His first attack occurred on February 22, when a masked gunman surprised Jimmy Hollis and Mary Jeanne Larey on a lonely lover's lane. He pistol-whipped both victims and sexually assaulted Larey, but left both victims alive. Others were not so fortunate. On March 24 the killer shot Richard Griffin and Polly Ann Moore on a road outside Texarkana. April 14 witnessed the lover's lane murder of Paul Martin and Betty Jo Booker. On May 3 the gunman changed tactics, invading the home of farmer Virgil Starks, killing him and wounding his wife before she escaped to seek help.

A prison psychiatrist, Dr. Anthony Lapolla, profiled the killer as a sexual sadist, but that brought police no closer to an arrest. Texas Rangers under Captain Manuel "Lone Wolf" Gonzaullas joined the manhunt, with FBI agents, Arkansas State Police, and sheriff's deputies from both sides of the border. Numerous suspects were questioned, Ranger marksmen staked out lover's lanes, and decoy couples—including male officers dressed as women—waited in vain for the killer's return.

national police force in occupied Japan, but Garrison declined, citing his duties as director of the DPS. He knew instinctively that Texas and its Rangers would require a steady guiding hand.

POSTWAR CRIME

Peacetime brought still more challenges for the Texas Rangers. The onset of a "cold war" between America and Russia sparked fears of

Hope flared briefly on May 5, when a man's corpse was found on nearby railroad tracks, sparking rumors that the killer had committed suicide. However, autopsy results proved that the man—Earl McSpadden—was stabbed to death and placed on the tracks. Police now believe he was slain by the Moonlight Murderer.

Captain Gonzaullas compiled a list of a dozen suspects, but none were linked to the crimes by hard evidence. Several published reports accuse career criminal Youell Swinney of the murders, noting that no further slayings occurred after his July 1946 arrest for auto theft. Swinney's wife joined in the accusations, but her story changed repeatedly and most investigators deemed her unreliable. Swinney denied involvement in the slayings but received a life prison term as a habitual offender. He was released in 1974, at age 57.

Captain Gonzaullas dismissed Swinney as a suspect in the Texarkana murders. Describing the manhunt as his most baffling case, Gonzaullas retired from the Rangers in 1951 but vowed to pursue the investigation as long as he lived. He died in 1977 with the case officially unsolved. The year before his death, a film titled *The Town That Dreaded Sundown* depicted the case with fictional details, including a shootout in which the wounded Phantom Killer escapes from Ranger Captain "J.D. Morales," portrayed by actor Ben Johnson.

RUSK STATE HOSPITAL SIEGE

Construction began on the East Texas Penitentiary at Rusk in 1877 and was completed in 1883. The facility housed convicts until it closed for renovation in 1917. Two years later it reopened as Rusk State Hospital for care of the "Negro insane." Six hundred patients were admitted during the first year, increasing to 2,308 by 1946. Along the way, other facilities were added, including a general hospital for care of the acutely ill, an infirmary for elderly invalids, separate tubercular wards for black and white patients, and a maximum-security unit for the criminally insane.[8]

On April 16, 1955, 81 inmates of the maximum-security unit overpowered hospital employees, seizing the hospital superintendent, his assistant supervisor, and a physician as hostages. Inmate spokesman Ben Riley complained that black inmates were often beaten by hospital staff, demanding equal treatment regardless of race, plus improved counseling and organized exercise periods. Newspaper coverage in the *Austin*

communist spying, while the state's first notorious serial killer terrorized Texarkana. The Rangers expanded to a force of 51 in 1947, and acquired their first airplane two years later, while the DPS opened new administrative offices and training facilities in Austin.

The 1950s, advertised by television long after the fact as "happy days," were a hectic era for the Texas Rangers. They averaged more than 8,000 investigations per year during the decade—16,571 in 1955 alone—and some were especially taxing.[9] Captain Robert Crowder peacefully resolved a hostage situation at the Rusk State Hospital for the criminally insane in 1955, while others quelled the violent Lone Star Steel strike at Daingerfield, two years later. Ranger Zeno Smith performed more traditional duties in Wilson County during July 1956, when he secured indictments against five cattle rustlers at Floresville.

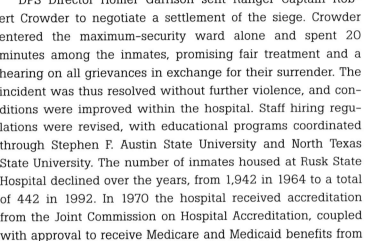

American reflects the atmosphere of racism, stating that the Rusk inmates had "no specific complaints" and describing Riley as the "leader of the gang of criminally insane Negroes" who "likes to exhibit his muscles."[10]

DPS Director Homer Garrison sent Ranger Captain Robert Crowder to negotiate a settlement of the siege. Crowder entered the maximum-security ward alone and spent 20 minutes among the inmates, promising fair treatment and a hearing on all grievances in exchange for their surrender. The incident was thus resolved without further violence, and conditions were improved within the hospital. Staff hiring regulations were revised, with educational programs coordinated through Stephen F. Austin State University and North Texas State University. The number of inmates housed at Rusk State Hospital declined over the years, from 1,942 in 1964 to a total of 442 in 1992. In 1970 the hospital received accreditation from the Joint Commission on Hospital Accreditation, coupled with approval to receive Medicare and Medicaid benefits from the U.S. Department of Health, Education, and Welfare.[11]

Violence flared throughout the South after May 1954, when the U.S. Supreme Court banned racial segregation in public schools. Texas was one of 15 states with separate schools for black and white students, and the Supreme Court's order stirred up passions reminiscent of secession and the Civil War. Racists shot three black teenagers in Mayflower, beat a civil rights worker to death in Gonzales, and bombed the Beaumont home of a white teacher working at an integrated college. In Houston, masked whites kidnapped an African American, whipped him with chains, and carved the letters "KKK" on his stomach.

The worst mob violence occurred in Mansfield, where hundreds of whites staged riots in August and September 1956. Federal courts had ordered integration of the local high school, but angry racists barred three minority students from enrolling, hung black effigies from nearby trees, beat bystanders, and threatened Tarrant County's sheriff when he tried to intervene. Armed men stopped cars approaching town, grilling drivers for their opinions on integration. Governor Allan Shivers, himself a segregationist, called the riots "an orderly protest" and sent Texas Rangers to ensure that no blacks entered Mansfield High School. Mansfield schools remained segregated until 1965, when they were threatened with the loss of federal funds.[12]

RANGERS MEET THE MOB

Cities have always harbored gangs, and members of foreign crime syndicates—the Sicilian Mafia, Italian Camorra, and Chinese tongs—arrived as immigrants during the 19th century, but America had no nationwide organized crime until Prohibition encouraged local gangs to unite in liquor smuggling. Gambling and other rackets soon were organized across state lines, as bloody gang wars left the strongest mobsters in charge.

In Texas, those were the Maceo brothers—Rosario ("Papa Rose"), Salvatore ("Sam"), and Vincent—barbers from Palermo, Sicily, who immigrated to Louisiana in 1901 and moved to Galveston in 1910. All members of the Mafia, they dabbled in crime until Texas went "dry" in 1918, then earned millions smuggling booze into Texas and shipping their surplus to other gangs nationwide. They operated from headquarters in Galveston's Hollywood Dinner Club from 1926 to 1939, when authorities finally closed it, then opened the Balinese Room in 1942 and continued wide-open gambling. Seven years later, when friends from the Cleveland Syndicate built the Desert Inn hotel-casino in Las Vegas, Nevada, the Maceos had a piece of the action.

Bribery kept Galveston police at bay while illegal casinos multiplied, prompting gamblers and reporters to call the island city the "Free State of Galveston."[13] Texas Rangers visited the club occasionally—greeted by a band playing *The Eyes of Texas Are Upon You*—but advance warning from local lawmen frustrated their investigations. Headline entertainers kept the showroom crowded, while suckers lost their money in the club's "secret" casino or spent it in 50 brothels with 1,000 prostitutes, lining nearby Post Office Street.[14]

"Godfather" Sam Maceo died in 1950, leaving Anthony Fertitta in charge of Galveston's rackets. Texas Attorney General Price Daniel indicted 23 Galveston mobsters in 1951, but a local judge dismissed all charges. The Mob ruled Galveston with little interference until 1957, when an embarrassing *Life* magazine article on "America's last surviving sin city" angered Attorney General Will Wilson. In June, Ranger Captain John Klevenhagen prepared a list of 65 casinos marked for raids, but corrupt police warned the targets. Finally, Klevenhagen warned Sheriff Frank Biaggne to "help us close the gambling dens or stay out of our way." Biaggne chose the latter course.[15]

Even so, it took three years to clean up Galveston. While two of Company A's eight Rangers spent their nights at the Balinese Room, keeping a watchful eye until it closed, others made their presence felt in different clubs. They also took advantage of a law that let police hold prisoners for three days without bail. One local mobster, nicknamed "Mad Dog," spent six months in jail on three-day raps, rearrested the moment his keepers released him from the previous bust. Gangsters shifted their gambling tables from place to place, but Rangers tracked them down, destroying equipment worth $2 million in June 1957 alone.[16]

It was too much for Anthony Fertitta. He moved to Las Vegas, leaving Texas in the hands of Dallas-based Joseph Civello's Mafia family—controlled, in turn, by Carlos Marcello from New Orleans. The Balinese Room survived as a legitimate nightclub until it finally closed in 2008.[17]

TURBULENT TIMES

The 1960s rocked America with racial and political unrest. The Texas Rangers, expanded to a force of 62 in 1961, often found themselves on the front line of social conflict.[18] A case in point was Crystal City, where Mexican Americans led by Juan Cornejo organized to crack Anglo dominance of politics and local schools. In 1963, Cornejo's Political Association of Spanish-speaking Organizations (PASSO) nominated five Hispanic candidates for city office and sought to unionize workers at a local fruit-packing plant. Anglo retaliation followed, and Rangers under Captain Alfred Allee were sent to supervise the election.

A Texas Ranger's equipment (circa 1965) consisted of a radio-dispatched, pursuit-type automobile; various types of firearms; nonlethal weapons for riot control; and crime detection gear. *(Bettmann/Corbis)*

Cornejo's candidates won their contests—and he was elected mayor—but trouble continued as Cornejo accused Captain Allee of physically assaulting him. Cornejo sued Allee, but the case was dismissed for lack of witnesses.[19] Meanwhile, personal quarrels within PASSO produced a new group, the Citizens Association Serving All Americans (CASSA), in 1964. Pledged to defeat politicians owned by "outside interests," CASSA won control of Crystal City's ruling council in 1965. Rangers returned to Crystal City in 1969, when a racial dispute over the selection of local high school cheerleaders threatened violence. A peaceful resolution was achieved, resulting in creation of the new Raza Unida (United Race) Party, whose members won seats on the city council and school board in 1970.[20]

A more serious incident brought Rangers to Houston's Texas Southern University (TSU) in 1967. Created specifically for African-American students in 1946, TSU experienced the same unrest as other segregated schools during the 1960s. In early 1967 members of the Student Nonviolent Coordinating Committee launched campus protests, citing alleged police brutality and other issues. Mass arrests followed, sparking violence on May 17 that left one policeman dead and 489 students in jail. Rangers helped restore order at TSU, and participated in the subsequent murder investigation. Five protest leaders were charged with inciting a riot resulting in death, but evidence produced at trial suggested the slain policeman was accidentally shot by other officers. Jurors failed to reach a verdict, and the charges were dismissed, leaving both sides unsatisfied.[21]

END OF AN ERA

Colonel Homer Garrison's influence in the state of Texas expanded throughout the 1960s. In 1963 Governor Connally chose Garrison to serve as chairman of the State Defense Council (in charge of both civil defense and disaster relief) *and* as director of the Governor's Highway

Three Visitors look at gun displays at the Texas Ranger Hall of Fame and Museum in Waco. (*AP Photo/*Waco Tribune-Herald, *Duane A. Laverty)*

Safety Commission. In May 1966 the Southern Region Highway Policy Committee of the Council of State Governments chose Garrison to serve as chairman of the group's resolution committee and as a member of its steering committee. January 1967 witnessed his appointment to the National Motor Vehicle Safety Advisory Council. Garrison's death, in May 1968, left Rangers wondering what would become of their agency and the DPS.[22]

Garrison's successor, Colonel Wilson Speir, joined the DPS as a highway patrolman in 1941, served with the U.S. Army Air Corps during World War II, and returned to the Highway Patrol in 1945. Speir and the DPS commissioners created new Criminal Law and Traffic Law Enforcement Divisions in 1968, while redefining Ranger duties to eliminate policing of labor disputes (as a result of the 1966–1967 farm workers' strike). In 1969 the Rangers expanded once more, to a force of 73 officers.[23]

Meanwhile, in 1968, a new Texas Ranger Hall of Fame and Museum opened in Waco, including the Garrison Gallery (with more than 14,000 Ranger artifacts, including some 2,500 historical firearms), the Texas Ranger Research Center, and headquarters for Ranger Company F.[24]

Modern Problems

Euless, Texas

On the night of October 13, 1971, Sergeant Bill Harvell made a routine traffic stop. The driver, Huron Walters, drew a pistol, but Harvell ducked behind the gunman's car before Walters could fire. As Walter sped away, Harvell fired several shots, then set off in high-speed pursuit.

During the chase, Walters fired at Harvell's cruiser, then ditched his car and vanished in the darkness. A 10-hour search proved fruitless, but officers uncovered Walters's 40-year criminal record. He had escaped from prison twice, and in the 1930s had served time with a member of Clyde Barrow's gang.[1]

At 7:30 A.M. on October 14, Hoyt Houston entered the garage of his Bedford, Texas, home and found Walters hiding there. Brandishing a shotgun, Walters took Houston, his wife, and their five-year-old daughter hostage. An older daughter heard the shouting and escaped through her bedroom window to call police.

When officers arrived, Walters ordered them to drop their guns, then forced his captives into their own car and sped off toward Rhome, 22 miles away. Halfway there, police cars forced the Houston's vehicle to stop. Surrounded, Walters raged and threatened to kill his hostages if he was not released. While local officers tried in vain to negotiate a peaceful resolution, Texas Ranger Tom Arnold watched Walters through the telescopic sight on his high-powered rifle.

At 8:03 A.M. Arnold saw that Walters seemed distracted by police moving around the hostage car. Taking advantage of the moment, Arnold fired a shot through the car's rear window, striking Walters in the head. The hostages immediately bolted from the car, while Walters remained inside. Unable to see through the shattered glass, Arnold ran forward, pistol drawn, shooting Walters three more times through a side window.[2]

Tarrant County's coroner pronounced Walters dead at the scene. Kate Houston suffered a scratch on one arm, from flying glass, but the family was otherwise unharmed.

NEW MANAGEMENT

Colonel Speir ran the DPS until his retirement on December 31, 1979. During his tenure, the department computerized more than 8 million driver and vehicle records and more than 1 million criminal records, and established a new communication system and a radio frequency reserved for Texas law enforcement officers. Speir also supervised hiring of the first female and minority DPS officers, although the Texas Rangers remained an all-male unit while he was in charge.[3]

Civil disorder from the 1960s continued into the new decade, as protest against the Vietnam War intensified. More than 20,000 demonstrators marched through Austin on May 5, 1970, protesting America's invasion of Cambodia. Texas Rangers joined local police and highway patrolmen for crowd-control duties—and inadvertently impounded Governor Preston Smith's car when he parked it illegally outside a restaurant.[4]

The Rangers kept expanding in the 1970s, their number increasing to 82 in 1971, then to 88 in 1974 and 94 in 1975. Recruitment and training standards also changed. New Rangers were accepted between the ages of 30 and 50, providing they had at least eight years of police experience and 400 to 600 hours of intermediate classroom instruction. Improved salaries, longevity pay, hospitalization benefits, and life insurance hastened evolution toward the status of an elite police agency.[5]

And the threat of violent crime persisted.

On July 24, 1974, inmates Fred Carrasco, Ignacio Cuevas, and Rudolfo Dominguez seized 81 hostages at Huntsville's state prison. The siege continued for 10 days, with Carrasco trading hostages for a television, handcuffs, and helmets manufactured in the prison's metal shop. Fifteen hostages remained on August 2, when the rebel convicts tried to escape in a crude "Trojan horse" built from materials found in the prison library. Ranger Captains G.W. Burks and Pete Rogers led an assault team that stopped the weird vehicle with high-pressure fire hoses. Carrasco committed suicide (by gun) and lawmen killed Dominguez and captured Cuevas unharmed. Two hostages also died in the battle, with one critically injured.[6]

Its border made Texas a frontline bastion of the 1970s "war on drugs." On February 20, 1978, Ranger Bobby Doherty joined DPS narcotics officers and local police on a drug raid in Denton. Suspect Gregory Ott shot Doherty in the head, killing him instantly. Ott received a life sentence and served 26 years before his parole in May 2004.[7]

James Adams, an ex-FBI agent and director of the Texas Criminal Justice Division, replaced Colonel Speir as DPS director in 1980, holding that office until June 1987. With successors Leo Gossett (June 1987 through July 1988) and Joe Milner (August 1988 through August 1991), he presided over an era of change for the Texas Rangers.

In the 1980s Rangers pursued more than 5,700 investigations and filed more than 3,200 criminal charges, ranging from old-fashioned livestock rustling to the sensational crimes of Henry Lucas and Ottis Toole. They arrested more than 1,200 suspects per year in that decade and recovered $8 million worth of stolen property, but success had its price.[8]

On January 14, 1987, parolee Brent Beeler kidnapped two-year-old Kara-Leigh Whitehead and her family's maid, Denise Johnson, from the Whitehead home in Horseshoe Bay. Eight days later, Beeler phoned the Whiteheads, demanding $30,000 ransom and a car for Kara-Leigh's safe return. At the January 22 ransom drop, Rangers John Aycock and Stanley Guffey hid in the car provided to Beeler. Surprised by the ambush, Beeler killed Guffey, while Aycock shot Beeler and pulled Kara-Leigh to safety. Police later found Denise Johnson's corpse at Beeler's rural hideout.[9]

CHANGING WITH THE TIMES

While historical records from 1839 name 130 Hispanics and 121 Native Americans as "Rangers," the tribesmen served only as scouts. A few

African Americans served the Rangers as teamsters (wagon drivers) during the 19th century, but none rated badges. From 1840 until 1969, Rangers were all white and male. Several women hired as Special Rangers in the 1930s served as "administrative assistants who handled especially sensitive information or security for the Governor," but they performed no investigative duties. Height requirements for Ranger applicants, established in 1935, served to bar most women and Asian or Hispanic men from filing applications. In the mid-1960s, when asked why there were no Asian-American Rangers, controversial Captain

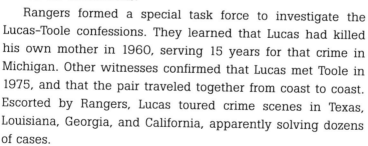

FALSE CONFESSIONS?

In June 1983 Texas Ranger Phil Ryan arrested ex-convict Henry Lucas (1936–2001) for illegal possession of firearms. Days later, Lucas confessed to killing his teenage girlfriend and an elderly woman in 1982. More confessions swiftly followed, until Lucas claimed more than 350 murders nationwide, starting in 1951. In many cases, Lucas claimed that he was joined by partner Ottis Toole (1947–1996). Already serving 20 years for arson in Florida, Toole—a self-described cannibal—confirmed the accusations.

Rangers formed a special task force to investigate the Lucas-Toole confessions. They learned that Lucas had killed his own mother in 1960, serving 15 years for that crime in Michigan. Other witnesses confirmed that Lucas met Toole in 1975, and that the pair traveled together from coast to coast. Escorted by Rangers, Lucas toured crime scenes in Texas, Louisiana, Georgia, and California, apparently solving dozens of cases.

In October 1983 a task force bulletin linked Lucas and Toole to 69 murders. A second announcement in January 1984 raised the total to 81, and by March 1985 police in 20 states had "cleared" 90 murders for Lucas alone, plus 28 for Toole and 109 committed by both men together. Lucas stood convicted in nine cases, including one death sentence, and was charged

Alfred Allee told a reporter, "We can't hire every doggone breed there is in the United States."[10]

On September 1, 1988, Sergeant Lee Roy Young Jr.—a 14-year DPS veteran—became the first black Texas Ranger. Earl Pearson soon joined the team as the Rangers' first black captain, later promoted to senior captain. By spring 1999, the Rangers claimed a total of six African-American officers.[11]

Beginning in the 1950s, lawsuits forced most American law enforcement agencies to drop minimum height requirements for hir-

in 30 more. Toole was convicted of two Florida killings and sentenced to die.

Then, in April 1985, Dallas reporter Hugh Aynesworth published a series of articles claiming that Lucas had lied about everything, using crime-scene details fed to him by over-zealous officers. The exposé was strange, since Aynesworth himself had proclaimed Lucas guilty in February 1985, but the stories caused Texas Attorney General Jim Mattox to accuse the Ranger task force of perpetrating a hoax. Some charges were dropped against Lucas, while others proceeded to trial and conviction. In 1991 Toole pled guilty to four Florida murders. Nationwide, authorities remain convinced that Lucas and Toole killed at least 100 victims during 1976–1983.

Lucas, meanwhile, recanted all of his confessions, even denying that he killed his mother. Toole persisted in confessing to various crimes, including the 1981 murder of Adam Walsh, six-year-old son of *America's Most Wanted* host John Walsh. In light of the uncertainty, in 1998 Governor George Bush commuted Lucas's death sentence to life imprisonment, clearly refusing to accept his claims of total innocence. Toole died in prison, from cirrhosis of the liver, on September 15, 1996. Lucas died from heart failure on March 13, 2001. Most of the crimes confessed by Lucas and Toole remain officially unsolved.

ing. The federal Crime Control Act of 1973 also required any police force with 50 or more employees, which received $25,000 or more in federal grants, to hire women or face loss of funding. Even so, the first two female Rangers—African-American Sergeant Christine Nix and Sergeant Cheryl Steadman, were not hired until 1993. Both confronted resistance from male Rangers. Sergeant Nix, a six-year DPS veteran, filed a lawsuit claiming sexual harassment in 1994, which resulted in four-month unpaid suspensions of Sergeant Matt Cawthon and Sergeant Jim Derman for addressing her with racist slurs. Sergeant Steadman resigned and filed a similar lawsuit in 1995, but the Texas Commission on Human Rights rejected her claim in January 1996.[12]

Art Rodriguez became the first Hispanic person to serve as a commissioned officer in the Texas Rangers in September 1969. By 2007, 21 were employed, including three captains, one lieutenant, and 16 sergeants. The only Asian-American Ranger, former Highway Patrol Sergeant Richard Shing, was accepted in 1993, when the Rangers hired female Sergeants Nix and Steadman.[13]

Art Rodriguez, center, is commissioned as the first Hispanic person to serve as an officer in the Texas Rangers in September 1969. Shown during the ceremony are, from left to right, Chief James M. Ray, Captain A.Y. Allee, Rodriguez, Colonel Wilson Speir, and Lieutenant Colonel Leo Gossett. *(AP Photo)*

RANGERS IN THE 1990s

DPS Directors James Wilson (1991–1996) and Dudley Thomas (1996–2000) led the Rangers through another era of challenge and change. In 1991 the Rangers became an official part of the director's staff, while the DPS Criminal Law Enforcement Division divided investigations between the Criminal Intelligence Service, the Motor Vehicle Theft Service, and the Narcotics Service. State legislators expanded the Rangers to 99 members in 1993, with increased salaries and fringe benefits.[14]

That same year found Rangers joining FBI agents in a standoff with the Branch Davidian religious cult at Mount Carmel, near Waco. A disastrous fire swept the cult's compound on April 19, claiming 76 lives, but one-third of the Ranger force remained in Waco for another three weeks, collecting more than 2,000 pieces of evidence. Ranger headquarters established its first computer system to catalog those items, as trials and investigations resulting from the siege dragged on through the year 2000.[15]

The Texas Rangers continued to grow, reaching 105 in 1996 and 107 (with two female Rangers) in 1999.[16] In 1997 they participated in another standoff with extremists, this one involving the self-styled "Republic of Texas." Sergeant Matt Cawthon investigated the Waco disappearance of Gary Peterson in 1997, determining that Peterson was murdered by his father-in-law, Sam Urick—a rogue ex-agent of the Central Intelligence Agency who once sold weapons to Libyan terrorists. Cawthon tracked Urick to Las Vegas, Nevada, and later pursued an accomplice to Honduras, where he captured the second killer with help from Ranger Lieutenant Clete Buckaloo. Urick received a life prison term, while the Honduran got 25 years.[17]

On Thanksgiving Day 1998, convicted killer Martin Gurule staged the first successful escape from death row in Texas since 1934. His breakout panicked Texans, and Rangers joined in the manhunt, but fear subsided on December 3, when Gurule was found drowned in a creek one mile from the prison.

Sergeant Matt Cawthon scored another victory in 1999, when he joined U.S. Postal Inspector Bob Adams and Detective Tom Noble from the Bellmead Police Department to crack a child-pornography ring in the Texas Hill Country. Eight defendants were convicted of producing

A Texas Ranger adds two rifles to a police vehicle trunk loaded with weapons confiscated from the vehicles of seven men being arrested in Pecos, Texas. The men were believed to have been trying to join 13 secessionists holed up in a remote mountain area. *(AP Photo/Eric Draper)*

child pornography and shipping it through the U.S. mail, resulting in long prison terms, while Cawthon, Adams, and Noble received Officer of the Year awards from Congress, the U.S. Department of Justice, the Fraternal Order of Police, and the National Center for Missing and Exploited Children.[18]

Another menace appeared in the form of Angel Maturino Reséndiz, a serial slayer nicknamed "the Railway Killer" for his habit of striking victims found near the railroads he traveled as a transient stowaway.

Various published accounts blame Reséndiz for 13 to 24 murders in Texas and four other states, committed between July 1991 and December 1998.[19] On June 21, 1999, the FBI added Reséndiz to its "Ten Most Wanted" list, but his days of freedom were already numbered.

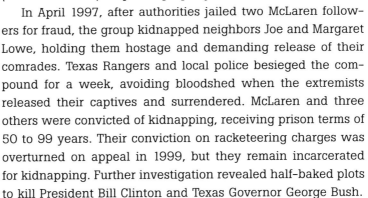

REPUBLIC OF TEXAS SIEGE (1997)

Some Texans claim their state is still an independent nation, never legally annexed by the United States. One such group, the "Republic of Texas," was founded in 1995, claiming 40,000 members ruled by an independent "provisional government." Personal quarrels split the group in 1996, producing three separate factions. Richard McLaren's group occupied a compound in the Davis Mountains and began harassing elected officials with nuisance lawsuits, fake arrest warrants, and liens (financial claims) on public property.

In April 1997, after authorities jailed two McLaren followers for fraud, the group kidnapped neighbors Joe and Margaret Lowe, holding them hostage and demanding release of their comrades. Texas Rangers and local police besieged the compound for a week, avoiding bloodshed when the extremists released their captives and surrendered. McLaren and three others were convicted of kidnapping, receiving prison terms of 50 to 99 years. Their conviction on racketeering charges was overturned on appeal in 1999, but they remain incarcerated for kidnapping. Further investigation revealed half-baked plots to kill President Bill Clinton and Texas Governor George Bush.

One splinter of the "Republic" still exists. Its Web site (http://texasrepublic.info/index.html) declares that "[t]he government of the republic of Texas Nation has now lawfully been vested back into the hands of the people of Texas as a constitutional republic nation. This process is not an act of seceding from the U.S. since history shows that citizens of the republic of Texas never voted to cede their land in the first place."[20]

Elected officials and the Texas Rangers disagree.

Texas Rangers arrest an unruly anti–death penalty demonstrator.
(Bob E. Daemmrich/Corbis)

Authorities identified Reséndiz's sister, Manuela, who agreed to help catch him alive in exchange for protective custody, visiting rights, and a psychiatric evaluation. Ranger Sergeant Drew Carter accompanied Manuela and a "spiritual advisor" to meet Reséndiz on the bridge between El Paso and Ciudad Juarez, Mexico, where Reséndiz surrendered to Carter on July 13, 1999. Charged with seven murders and convicted of one in May 1999, Reséndiz received a death sentence in Texas and was executed by lethal injection on June 27, 2006.

21ST-CENTURY RANGERS

DPS Director Thomas Davis led the Rangers into their third century, with Senior Captain Bruce Casteel commanding 107 officers.[21] Four years later, in May 2004, Earl Pearson became the Rangers' first African-American senior captain, appointed as Chief of the Ranger Division. Cases pursued by the Rangers in the first decade of the 21st century include the following:

- *January 2005*: Two Willacy County commissioners, Jose Jimenez and Israel Tamez, were convicted of accepting bribes from fellow commissioner David Cortez. Cortez pled guilty to arranging the bribes for local contractors. Jimenez received a six-month sentence, while Cortez was sentenced to three months. Tamez died prior to sentencing.[22]
- *April 2007*: Rangers investigated sexual assault charges filed against Corpus Christi Police Chief Bryan Smith by a former girlfriend. Smith denied the accusation and was later reassigned to replace the city's retiring police commander in 2008.[23]
- *August 2007*: Rangers and FBI agents arrested former Nacogdoches County Jail administrator Michael Kennedy for distributing child pornography. In March 2008 Kennedy received a 97-month prison term.[24]
- *February 2008*: Ranger Trace McDonald and DPS Criminal Intelligence Agent Michael Adcock arrested methamphetamine dealer John Downing in Henderson County, on drug and parole violation charges.[25]

- *April 2008*: Rangers and other authorities raided a polygamist compound at Eldorado, after receiving reports of alleged child abuse and forced marriage of minors to middle-aged men. More than 400 children were removed for safekeeping, but most were later returned to the compound, while Rangers pursued investigation of false abuse reports.[26]
- *May 2008*: Rangers investigated the fatal police shooting of Kenneth Crosby, in Electra. No charges were filed.[27]
- *December 2008*: Rangers investigated a municipal court clerk in Italy, Texas, on suspicion of mishandling town funds and engaging in nepotism (unlawful favoritism toward relatives).[28]
- *December 2008*: After the shooting of a teenager in San Saba, Rangers and agents of the Texas Alcoholic Beverage Commission arrested Alexandra Rhodes on charges of furnishing liquor to minors, aggravated assault, and deadly conduct.[29]
- *March 2009*: Rangers investigated charges that a police officer in Rosebud choked a teenager during a routine traffic stop. The officer resigned, while claiming self-defense.[30]
- *April 2009*: Rangers began investigating the unexplained death of an inmate at the Webb County jail. Rodolofo Moreno died in his cell overnight, but deputies found no apparent cause. During the course of that investigation, Rangers arrested Deputy Sheriff Alejandro Avila on unrelated felony theft charges.[31]

With those investigations and more in progress, changes in the Rangers' upper ranks continued. Stanley Clark replaced Tom Davis as DPS director in September 2008, while Lieutenant Colonel Lamar Beckworth became the department's first African-American assistant director and Antonio Leal became the first Hispanic senior captain of the Texas Rangers. Clark's tenure was brief, however, as a female employee's accusation of sexual harassment and unprofessional conduct forced his resignation on May 5, 2009. Lamar Beckworth replaced Clark as interim director, with promotion to the rank of colonel.[32]

RANGERS TODAY

The modern Texas Rangers are divided into six companies, A through F, with headquarters in Austin, plus San Antonio's Unsolved Crimes

Texas Rangers Captain Barry Caver responds to questions at a press conference after authorities moved to search the large white temple on the polygamist compound of the Fundamentalist Church of Jesus Christ of Latter Day Saints in Eldorado, Texas. *(AP Photo/ Tony Gutierrez)*

Investigation Team. Felony crimes are still the Rangers' main focus, often working in cooperation with the DPS Criminal Intelligence Service (on gambling cases), the Motor Vehicle Theft Service (on cases including thefts of heavy equipment), and the Narcotics Service (on drug cases).

All modern Rangers applicants must have at least eight years' experience in law enforcement, including four years with the Texas DPS. They must also have at least 60 hours of college education or an approved equivalent, display skill with firearms, and perform successfully on competitive written tests and interviews. On average, each Ranger vacancy produces 150 to 200 applications from hopeful candidates.[33]

Those chosen receive training in fingerprint recovery, photography, blood-spatter analysis, investigative hypnosis, and other crime-detection skills. Each Ranger is required to attend 40 hours of in-service training every two years, but most exceed that minimum demand.

Unlike the old days, when each Ranger supplied his own horse and equipment, the state now provides modern vehicles and crime-fighting gear. Each Ranger receives a laptop computer, digital and video cameras, audio recorders, a cellular telephone, a fingerprinting kit, materials for casting footprints or other impressions, and a black light for spotting trace evidence invisible to the naked eye.

More traditional tools include semiautomatic pistols (a choice of the .357 Magnum SIG P226 Elite or a Colt .45), a 12-gauge shotgun, and a Ruger Mini-14 rifle. Each Ranger also receives a gas mask, helmet, body armor, riot baton, handcuffs, and shackles. Each Ranger company's backup arsenal includes sniper rifles and night-vision scopes, automatic weapons, tear-gas guns, and other "less lethal" weapons.

One thing about the Rangers still remains unchanged. Each officer selects his or her own clothing, within broad general guidelines. Western-style wear is traditional, including a white cowboy hat and boots. For SWAT-type tactical situations, Rangers wear black military-style fatigue uniforms with an embroidered shoulder patch.

Senior Captain Antonio Leal sums up the Ranger team:

These highly motivated men and women, selected from many outstanding candidates, take pride in the colorful traditions they have inherited and the modern challenges they face. As living symbols of a unique heritage, they wear the boots, white hats, and pistol belts of their predecessors. As elite law enforcement officers of the 21st century, they have added college degrees, networked computers, cell phones, and state-of-the-art forensic analyses. The Texas Rangers [have] a heritage to be valued and [are] a symbol of service for future generations.[34]

Ranger Heroes

Tres Jacales, Mexico

In the early 1890s, Jesus-Maria Olguin and his son Severio led a gang of Mexican outlaws that terrorized ranches in El Paso County, Texas, stealing livestock for sale across the border. Operating from the town of Tres Jacales, on Pirate Island in the middle of the Rio Grande, the Olguin gang was legally untouchable by law enforcement officers from the United States.

But technicalities did not faze Captain Frank Jones of the Texas Rangers.

On June 30, 1893, Jones crossed the river to Pirate Island with Ranger Privates Ed Aten, Carl Kirchner, J. Wood Saunders, and T.F. Tucker, plus El Paso County Deputy Sheriff R.E. Bryant. After searching the Olguin home and finding it deserted, they met two armed riders who turned and fled at sight of the lawmen. Jones and the rest pursued them to Tres Jacales, where the bandits dismounted and ducked into an adobe building.

As the officers drew near, gunfire erupted around them, weapons firing from the town and from the surrounding brush. A bullet struck Captain Jones in the thigh and knocked him from his saddle. He continued firing from the ground, until another bullet pierced his chest. As Private Tucker approached, ducking gunfire, Jones called out, "Boys I'm shot all to pieces. I'm killed. Save yourselves!"[1]

Reluctantly, still taking fire, the survivors retreated, leaving Jones dead on the ground. El Paso County Sheriff Frank Simmons traveled to Ciudad Juarez, seeking the return of Jones's body, and Mexican authorities released it with his personal effects, after several days of diplomatic wrangling. The Olguins were reportedly arrested after a shootout with Mexican troops, but they were never prosecuted for killing Captain Jones. Relatives buried Jones at a ranch owned by his father-in-law, but he was exhumed and reburied at Ysleta in 1936, with a state historical marker telling his story.

FAST GUNS AND STEADY AIM

For all of their modern achievements, Texas Rangers are most famous for a long tradition of facing down outlaws in deadly combat, trading shot for shot with some of the Wild West's most notorious gunmen. Since 1837, 91 Rangers have been murdered by felons resisting arrest.[2] Others—including most of those inducted to the Texas Ranger Hall of Fame—are honored for their icy nerve and deadly marksmanship in battle with Indian warriors, Mexican troops and guerrillas, rustlers and bandits, bank robbers, and kidnappers.

They are the shooting stars of Texas, models of the Ranger tradition, revered as heroes despite—or because of—the controversies some inspired during their lives as lawmen on the wild frontier.

JOHN B. JONES (1834–1881)

A native of South Carolina, Jones moved to Texas with his parents at age four. He began his college education at LaGrange, Texas, and finished it in South Carolina, returning in time to join Benjamin Terry's Eighth Texas Cavalry—better known as Terry's Texas Rangers—when the Civil War began in 1861. Jones later transferred to the Fifteenth Texas Infantry and finished the war as a major.

Still devoted to the failed Confederacy after Appomattox, Jones toured Mexico in 1865, hoping to start an expatriate rebel colony, but he soon gave up that effort and returned to Texas. White voters sent him to the state legislature in 1868, but his persistent defense of secession prompted "radical" Republicans to prevent him from serving. Six years later, when Texas was restored to the Union and a new Frontier Battalion of Texas Rangers was formed, Governor Richard Coke placed Jones in charge with the rank of major.

On July 12, 1874, Jones led 40 Rangers to meet Chief Lone Wolf and 125 Indian warriors at Lost Valley. His best efforts failed to halt the San Elizario "salt war" in 1877, but in July of that same year he negotiated a truce in the bloody Horrell-Higgins feud. In January 1879, while retaining his post as commander of the Frontier Battalion, Jones assumed the added duty of serving as adjutant general of the State of Texas. He married late in life, in February 1879, and died in Austin from natural causes while still in active service, on July 19, 1881.

Ranger historian Frederick Wilkins says of Major Jones: "It would be difficult to overstate Jones' importance in the development of the Rangers . . . [He] put his brand on the form and style of discipline, morale and conduct. He set the standard for administration . . . Jones developed a business-like fighting force which he personally supervised, riding up and down the frontier each year . . . [H]e never lost his love for his men . . . he knew each officer and noncommissioned officer and many of the privates . . . Without him the Rangers would probably have been dissolved, and it is a tribute to him that in his day he was known, admired and respected as *the* Texas Ranger."[3]

LAWRENCE SULLIVAN ROSS (1838–1898)

"Sul" Ross was born in newly formed Iowa Territory, eight years before statehood, and moved to Texas with his family before his first birthday. He attended Baylor University at Independence, Texas, then transferred to Alabama's Wesleyan University. During the summer of his junior year, Ross joined the U.S. Army to command a company of Native American soldiers on the Brazos Indian Reservation and suffered a serious wound from hostile Comanches in October 1858. Nonetheless, he recovered in time to graduate from Wesleyan in the spring of 1859.

Back in Texas during 1860, Ross joined the Rangers and participated in Captain Middleton Johnson's campaign against the Comanches that December. While it failed to suppress hostile raiders, that campaign did liberate captive Cynthia Parker, kidnapped by Comanche raiders 20 years earlier. Ross quit the Rangers when the Civil War began in 1861 to serve as the state's peace commissioner to various Indian tribes, then joined a Confederate Army company formed by his older brother in Waco. Rising through the ranks to serve as a major, then colonel, Ross fought in battles at Pea Ridge, Arkansas, and at Corinth and Vicksburg, Mississippi. War's end found him a brigadier general, commanding the Twenty-Seventh Texas Calvary.

The war sapped Ross's health, and he spent the Reconstruction era as a farmer, fathering six children. Rampant crime in McLennan County persuaded Ross to serve as sheriff during 1873–1875, during which time he helped organize the Sheriffs' Association of Texas. Voters elected him to the state senate in 1880 and to the first of two terms as governor in 1886. Ross retired from politics in 1891, to serve as president of the financially troubled Agricultural and Mechanical College of Texas (now Texas A & M University). He held that post until his sudden death, on January 3, 1898. Sul Ross State University in Alpine, Texas, is named in his honor.

WILLIAM JESSE MCDONALD (1852–1918)

One of the Texas Rangers' "Four Great Captains," Bill McDonald never really planned on a career in law enforcement. A Mississippi native who moved west with his family after the Civil War, he faced treason charges after a clash with Union soldiers in 1868 but was acquitted. McDonald graduated from a New Orleans commercial college in 1872 and taught penmanship in Henderson, Texas, while operating small stores at Brown's Bluff and Mineola.

When his business ventures faltered, McDonald sought to supplement his income as a lawman, serving first as a Wood County deputy sheriff, then shifting to a similar job in Hardeman County, before he became a Special Ranger and U.S. Deputy Marshal, patrolling northern Texas and southern Kansas. He showed more talent for police work than commerce, capturing rustlers and train robbers, driving the Brooken Gang out of Hardeman County, and soon acquiring status as a living legend in the Cherokee Strip.

In 1891, Governor James Hogg chose McDonald to lead Company B of the Frontier Battalion. Two years later, he nearly died in a shootout with corrupt Childress County Sheriff John Matthews. McDonald

(Continued on page 94)

FRANK HAMER (1884–1955)

Thanks to Hollywood's production of *Bonnie and Clyde* (1967), Frank Hamer may be the most famous real-life Texas Ranger of all time. The film's producers are lucky that Hamer died before its release, however, since its false portrayal of him as a bungler who was captured by the outlaw lovers, then stalked and killed them for personal revenge, might have sparked his anger.

And Francis Augustus Hamer was deadly when riled.

Counting Clyde Barrow and Bonnie Parker, Hamer killed 53 adversaries during his 43 years as a lawman—a dozen more than the score normally credited to Texas gunfighter John Wesley Hardin.[4] Unlike Hardin's tally, however, those slain by Hamer were all armed felons with histories of violence.

A Texas native, Hamer grew up on a ranch and worked as a cowboy until April 1906, when he joined the Rangers at age 22. By then, he had survived one gunfight, while his opponent did not. Farmer Dan McSwain offered Hamer $150 to kill a troublesome neighbor, then threatened Hamer's life when Frank refused. Two days later, McSwain shot Hamer from ambush. Upon recovering, Hamer confronted McSwain and killed him in a classic showdown.[5]

As a Ranger, Hamer patrolled the border for two years, then resigned to serve as Navasota's city marshal during 1908–1911. Next, Hamer enforced the law as a Harris County special officer, before rejoining the Rangers in 1915. He took another break at the start of Prohibition, serving briefly as a federal "dry" agent, then joined the Rangers a third time in 1921, winning promotion to senior captain in January 1922. The Roaring Twenties kept him busy in various oil towns, but in 1928 he also challenged the Texas Bankers Association, demonstrating that their $5,000 reward for dead bandits had prompted the framing and murder of various small-time criminals.

Hamer was among the Rangers who resigned to protest Governor "Ma" Ferguson's election in 1932, but two years later he was hired as special investigator for the Texas prison system, to crush the Barrow–Parker gang by any means necessary. Hamer achieved that goal in May 1934, when his posse killed Bonnie and Clyde in a blizzard of gunfire near Gibsland, Louisiana. For that achievement, Hamer received a special citation from Congress.

Over the next 24 years, Hamer worked for various Texas oil companies as a strikebreaker. Labor unions condemned him as a hired thug, while management praised him for preventing strike-related violence. In 1948 Governor Coke Stevenson persuaded Hamer to don a Ranger badge for the fourth time,

(continues)

Four members of the six-man posse that ambushed and killed fugitive criminals Clyde Barrow and Bonnie Parker sit for a photograph on the day after the ambush. Pictured, from left to right, are Dallas County Sheriff's Deputies Bob Alcorn and Ted Hinton and Texas Rangers B.M. "Manny" Gault and Captain Frank Hamer. (*Getty Images*)

(continued)

supervising state elections in the corrupt precincts of Duval and Jim Wells Counties. Hamer retired for the last time in 1949 and died in Austin on July 10, 1955. Shortly before his death, he told his son, "I've killed 52 men and one woman, but I sleep every night knowing I did right."[6]

In 1967 Hamer's widow and son sued *Bonnie and Clyde*'s producers for disgracing Hamer's memory. After four years of legal maneuvers, the defendants settled out of court for an undisclosed amount.[7]

(Continued from page 91)

persevered as a Ranger captain until 1907, earning a fabled reputation as "a man who would charge Hell with a bucket of water."[8] His famous activities include prevention of the Fitzsimmons-Maher prize fight in El Paso, solution of a Wichita Falls bank robbery and the Conditt family murders near Edna, exposure of the San Saba "Murder Society," suppression of the Reese-Townsend feud at Columbus, and investigation of the Brownsville Raid in 1906.

McDonald left the Rangers to become a state revenue agent in January 1907 and reprised his role as a U.S. Deputy Marshal in northern Texas from 1912 until pneumonia claimed his life on January 15, 1918.

JOHN ABIJAN BROOKS (1855–1944)

Another of the Rangers' "Four Great Captains," Brooks was born in Kentucky, working as a miner and cowboy before he reached Texas at age 21. He joined the Rangers as a private in January 1883, and nearly lost his own life three years later, battling outlaws in Indian Territory (now Oklahoma). A month later, he killed a cowboy in a gunfight at Alex, Oklahoma, and was convicted of manslaughter, but fellow Rangers secured a pardon from President Grover Cleveland, permitting Brooks to rejoin the Rangers.

On March 31, 1887, Rangers fought a pitched battle with the Conner Gang, a criminal clan in Sabine County. Private James Moore was killed, while Captain William Scott and Private John Rogers were wounded. Sergeant Brooks lost three fingers, but remained in service. The Conners escaped that day but were killed while resisting arrest in autumn 1887.

Brooks continued rising through the Ranger ranks, to command Company F as a captain in 1889. He patrolled various oil boomtowns in eastern and southern Texas, prevented an outlawed prize fight at Galveston in 1901, and arrested five suspects in the 1902 murder of Ranger Sergeant A.Y. Baker. He resigned in November 1906 and later served in the state legislature, then as a judge in Brooks County (named in his honor) from 1911 to 1939. Brooks died from kidney failure on January 15, 1944.

JOHN REYNOLDS HUGHES (1855–1947)

Number three among the Rangers' "Four Great Captains," John Hughes was born in Illinois and left home at age 14 to become a cowboy. That trade led him to Texas in 1874, after six years in Indian Territory, and he bought a ranch in Travis County. In 1886, Hughes pursued a band of rustlers from Texas to New Mexico, killing several and capturing the rest. In July 1887, while still a civilian, he helped Ranger Ira Aten track and arrest fugitive murderer Judd Roberts.

Those exploits earned him an invitation to join the Texas Rangers, which he accepted in August 1887. Promoted to sergeant by 1893, he took command of Company D as its captain in July of that year, after members of the Olguin gang killed Captain Frank Jones on Pirate Island. When the Frontier Battalion was dissolved in 1901, Hughes stayed on as a captain, commanding Company D in the new Ranger force. Known as "the border boss" for his pursuit of rustlers, murderers, and silver thieves around the Shafter mines, Hughes retired in January 1915, as the longest-serving Texas Ranger.[9]

The year before his retirement, author Zane Grey had dedicated his novel *The Lone Star Ranger* to Hughes and his men. Hughes spent his later years prospecting, touring the Southwest, and serving as chairman of Austin's Citizens Industrial Bank. In 1940 he received the first

Certificate of Valor, created to honor American peace officers. Hughes committed suicide in Austin on June 3, 1947.[10]

IRA ATEN (1862–1953)

The son of an Illinois minister, Ira Aten moved to Texas with his family at age 14. Two years later, he witnessed the Ranger slaying of outlaw Sam Bass and pledged himself to become a lawman. Aten joined the Frontier Battalion in March 1883, serving first as a private under Captain L.P. Seiker, and later as a sergeant under Captain Frank Jones.

"LONE WOLF" GONZAULLAS (1891–1977)

Manuel Trazazas Gonzaullas was born at Cádiz, Spain, while his Spanish father and Canadian mother—both naturalized American citizens—were visiting his father's homeland. At age 20, in 1911, Gonzaullas attained the rank of major in the Mexican army, resigning in 1915 to become an agent of the U.S. Treasury Department. He switched careers again in 1920, joining the Texas Rangers, and acquired his famous nickname in December of that year from an article in the *Wichita Falls Daily Times*. That story, published on December 29, reported that the bootleggers, gamblers, and drug smugglers Gonzaullas stalked along the Tex-Mex border knew him as *El Lobo Solo*— "the lone wolf," in Spanish—because he was a solitary manhunter.[11]

At Kilgore, in 1931, Gonzaullas confronted one of the state's worst wide-open boomtowns. As Gonzaullas recalled, "There was no police department—it didn't exist. . . . Things were very bad and we had to have a jail of some sort and we didn't have one. So I went down to the hardware store and I secured . . . a chain, oh I guess it was a city block long . . . and I took this here chain and I put about a hundred trace chains on it. I put padlocks on the trace chains and . . . I opened a little jail in kind of a seed store . . . . We put the men on [one] end with the chains around the men's necks and we put the women on

In July 1887, aided by future Ranger John Hughes, Aten tracked and captured murderer Judd Roberts, a member of Butch Cassidy's Wild Bunch. The following year, Aten used explosive booby traps to frustrate illegal fence cutters in Navarro County. In 1889, Governor Lawrence Ross sent Aten and a Ranger squad to quell Fort Bend County's Jaybird-Woodpecker War, a political feud between racist white Democrats ("Jaybirds") and Republicans who supported black suffrage. The fighting claimed at least three lives before Aten's Rangers suppressed it, resulting in a declaration of martial law.[12] Local authorities were so

the opposite end. We'd put the chains on the women's ankle with a padlock on it. And we never lost any . . . . And of course when they wanted to go to the rest room or anything, why they just passed the bucket."[13]

Despite his enviable record of suppressing crime in southern Texas, Gonzaullas was among the Rangers fired by Governor Miriam Ferguson in January 1933. When rampant corruption prompted legislators to create a new Department of Public Safety in 1935, Gonzaullas was picked to lead that agency's Bureau of Intelligence. In that post, he promoted development of a crime laboratory which ranked second only to the FBI's famous lab in Washington, D.C.

Still, Lone Wolf Gonzaullas missed frontline, crime-fighting action. In February 1940 he quit the DPS Bureau of Intelligence to serve as captain of Texas Ranger Company B, based in Dallas. While he worked many cases in the next decade, the most famous—and most baffling—was his pursuit of Texarkana's "Moonlight Murderer" in 1946. Gonzaullas retired in 1951, serving as a technical consultant on movies, radio and television programs dealing with the Texas Rangers. In 1968 he helped create the Texas Ranger Hall of Fame and Museum, leaving his scrapbooks and personal papers to that institution when he died on February 13, 1977.

impressed with Aten that they persuaded him to leave the Rangers and become Fort Bend County's sheriff.

From there, in 1893, Aten moved on to serve as Castro County's sheriff, then turned vigilante to hunt rustlers for the Capitol Syndicate Company in 1895. Backed by a 20-man "ranch police force," including ex-Rangers Ed Connell and Wood Saunders, Aten pursued that trade until 1904, when he moved his family to California.[14] Entering local politics in 1923, Aten published his memoirs 22 years later, and died of pneumonia at age 91 on August 5, 1953.

JOHN HARRIS ROGERS (1863–1930)

The last of the "Four Great Captains" was a Texas native who joined the Rangers in 1882. John Rogers suffered gunshot wounds battling the Conners Gang in March 1887, but lived to serve as a sergeant under Captain John Brooks, and was promoted to captain in 1892. While enforcing a smallpox quarantine at Laredo, Rogers survived another gunshot wound requiring surgical removal of bone splinters from one arm. That injury forced Rogers to use a specially made Winchester rifle, but it did not spoil his aim.

Before leaving the Rangers in January 1911, Rogers tracked and arrested the usual collection of bandits, rustlers, and murderers. Upon retiring, Rogers became an elder of the Presbyterian Church and a tireless campaigner against alcohol, delivering temperance lectures with a Bible in one hand and a pistol on his hip.[15]

In 1913, President Woodrow Wilson appointed Rogers to serve as a U.S. Deputy Marshal in western Texas. Rogers held that post until 1921, when he accepted appointment as Austin's police chief. Governor Dan Moody persuaded Rogers to resume his duties as a Ranger captain in 1927. He was still in service when he died from complications of gall bladder surgery at Temple, Texas, on November 11, 1930.

ROBERT GOSS (1898–1978)

A Texas native, born at Honey Grove, Bob Goss nurtured a childhood love of guns that never waned. He often told acquaintances, "You're not serious about shooting until you've fired at least a million rounds," and most agreed that Goss had fired many times that number of bullets—sometimes at other men.[16]

Goss joined the Texas Rangers in June 1924, earning a reputation for lethal marksmanship in various oil boomtowns. However, while historian Robert Nieman calls Goss "the deadliest gun in the Rangers," no tally of his kills exists and there is no evidence suggesting that he rivaled the toll of colleague Frank Hamer.[17]

Aside from cleaning up wide-open towns, Goss policed Sherman, Texas, during its May 1930 race riot, enforced closure of a controversial toll bridge built between Texas and Oklahoma the following year, and spent so much time as a bodyguard for Captain Manuel "Lone Wolf" Gonzaullas that fellow rangers dubbed him "Shadow" Goss. His spare time was filled with target practice and shooting exhibitions that included blasting the pips from playing cards with a .45-caliber pistol (sometimes with the gun held upside-down).

Goss quit the Rangers in 1934, spending two years as Kilgore's chief of police, but later returned to serve through most of the 1940s. He died in Kilgore on March 8, 1978, five months shy of his 80th birthday.

Fictional Rangers

Somewhere in Texas

Outlaws surround a lonely farmhouse, pouring rifle fire through doors and windows while members of the family inside try to defend themselves. One of the gunmen rushes toward a wagon filled with hay, meant for the farmer's livestock, and sets it afire, using the wagon and its rising cloud of smoke for cover as he shoves it toward the house. Soon, those inside will be trapped, with no hope of escape.

But suddenly, a solitary figure on a great white stallion charges in among the badmen, firing six-guns left and right. His aim is so precise that each shot blasts a bandit's weapon out of action, without wounding—much less killing—any of the would-be murderers. In seconds flat, the rider has his enemies disarmed and cowering. The farmer and his family emerge to sweep the outlaws' guns away and bind their hands.

That job is barely done, when the farmer's wife sees that their savior is gone, vanished as swiftly and mysteriously as he came. "Who was that man?" she asks. "We never even had a chance to thank him!"

"Never mind," her husband says, smiling. "That was the Lone Ranger."

RANGERS THAT NEVER WERE

Worldwide, there is little more than a handful of truly famous law enforcement agencies. They include the FBI, Canada's Mounties, Lon-

Clayton Moore played The Lone Ranger in 169 episodes of the 1950s television series. *(John Springer Collection/Corbis)*

don's Scotland Yard, LAPD, NYPD . . . and the Texas Rangers. Others—Chicago's police or Miami's, California's Highway Patrol, the U.S. Secret Service, even tiny Selma, Alabama's sheriff—are famous in spurts, for some headline-making case or scandal, but they do not rush to mind when crime fighting is mentioned.

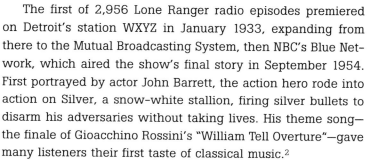

THE LONE RANGER

No fictional lawman is more famous than the Lone Ranger, sole survivor of an outlaw ambush that killed his brother and four other Texas Rangers. Gravely wounded, he lies near death until rescued by a Native American tribesman named Tonto ("stupid" or "silly" in Spanish).[1] Upon recovering, the Ranger dons a mask and rides off with Tonto in pursuit of justice, capturing criminals and defending the innocent wherever they are found.

The first of 2,956 Lone Ranger radio episodes premiered on Detroit's station WXYZ in January 1933, expanding from there to the Mutual Broadcasting System, then NBC's Blue Network, which aired the show's final story in September 1954. First portrayed by actor John Barrett, the action hero rode into action on Silver, a snow-white stallion, firing silver bullets to disarm his adversaries without taking lives. His theme song—the finale of Gioacchino Rossini's "William Tell Overture"—gave many listeners their first taste of classical music.[2]

The Lone Ranger galloped onto the movie screen with short features in September 1920 (also called *The Unknown Ranger*) and December 1927. Republic Pictures launched the first Lone Ranger serial in February 1938, with 15 weekly chapters that left the masked Ranger (and the actor who played him) forever

While the FBI under J. Edgar Hoover (1895–1972) ran more sophisticated public-relations campaigns, often taking credit for cases solved by other agencies, the Texas Rangers had an 85-year head start on the famous "G-Men." Two novels dealing with the Rangers—A.W. Arrington's *The Rangers and Regulators* and *Bernard Lile* by Jere Clemens—were published in 1856. Hundreds more have followed, including popular series penned by authors Louis L'Amour, Elmer Kelton, James Griffin, Kjell Hallbing (writing as "Louis Masterson"), and Larry McMurtry.

unnamed. A second serial, *The Lone Ranger Rides Again,* premiered in February 1939 with actor Robert Livingston in the title role.[3]

Television welcomed the Lone Ranger in September 1949, airing the first of 221 half-hour episodes starring Clayton Moore in the title role, with Jay Silverheels cast as Tonto. Moore and Silverheels also made three feature films: *The Legend of the Lone Ranger* (1952), *The Lone Ranger* (1956), and *The Lone Ranger and the Lost City of Gold* (1958). Their TV series closed in June 1957, and a 1961 attempt to revive it as *The Return of the Lone Ranger,* with Tex Hill starring, did not survive past the pilot broadcast.[4]

King Features Syndicate also distributed a Lone Ranger comic strip in newspapers from September 1938 to December 1971, while Dell Comics published 145 Lone Ranger comic books between 1948 and 1962.

When the Lone Ranger returned to theaters in 1981, actor Klinton Spilsbury portrayed a darker hero, who showed no mercy to his brother's killers. While the film was not a great success—it earned five Razzie Awards for Worst Picture, Worst Actor, and so on—the franchise survives. A new Lone Ranger film is scheduled for release in 2012, reportedly starring Johnny Depp as Tonto.[5]

Beginning in October 1936, authors of Texas Ranger novels faced stiff competition from *Texas Rangers Magazine,* one of many American "pulp" magazines, so called for their use of cheap wood-pulp paper. From its debut until the magazine ceased publication in February 1958, each of its 206 issues featured an adventure tale starring Ranger Jim Hatfield, written by various authors using the pen name "Jackson Cole." Aside from the novel-length feature story, each issue also contained short stories by various authors, including best-seller Louis L'Amour writing as "Jim Mayo."[6]

Collector Jim Griffin has identified 12 authors who used the Cole name while writing for *Texas Rangers Magazine.* Leslie Scott and Tom Curry each wrote 55 Hatfield adventures, while Walker Tompkins wrote 32, Roe Richmond wrote 22, Peter Germano wrote 16, Dwight Newton wrote four, Joseph Chadwick wrote three, Clark Gray wrote two, and single stories were authored by C. William Harrison, Dean Owen, Lin Searles, and Lee Wells. The authors of 13 other Hatfield stories remain unidentified today.[7]

Fictional Rangers are not always hard-riding, fast-drawing heroes, by any means. In recent years, they have conquered the realm of best-selling romance novels, including such examples as Jan Hudson's *The Texas Ranger* (2007), Patricia Thayer's *The Texas Ranger Takes a Bride* (2008), Tina Leonard's *Texas Ranger Twins* (2009), and Carol Finch's *Texas Ranger, Runaway Heiress* (2009).

HOLLYWOOD RANGERS

Texas Rangers leaped from the printed page onto movie screens in April 1910, with the release of *The Ranger's Bride,* starring Gilbert "Bronco Billy" Anderson. Over the next 99 years—by the time *American Cartel* reached theaters in April 2009—Rangers had featured prominently in 214 motion pictures.[8]

Many of those films were traditional Western adventures, but others offered surprises—and sometimes inspired controversy. Hollywood's depiction of Ranger Captain Frank Hamer in *Bonnie and Clyde* (1967) sparked criticism and spawned a lawsuit, which the producers settled out of court. Actor Dennis Hopper portrayed a mentally unbalanced Ranger obsessed with revenge in *Texas Chainsaw Massacre 2* (1986), while Jack Yates's "Colonel Hammer" invaded Vietnam to find his missing brother in *Phantom Soldiers* (1987). "Captain Tom Pickett" (played by Ken Jenkins) strikes a dangerous bargain with gangster John Smith (Bruce Willis) in *Last Man Standing* (1996).

Some actors have a particular fondness for portraying Texas Rangers. Writer/director/producer Quentin Tarantino cast Michael Parks as Ranger Earl McGraw in three completely unrelated films: *From Dusk Till Dawn* (1996), *Kill Bill Vol. 1* (2003), and *Planet Terror* (2007). Chuck Norris first wore a Ranger's badge as the title character in *Lone Wolf*

McQuade (1983), then portrayed Ranger Cordell Walker in a popular television series, *Walker, Texas Ranger*, and three made-for-TV movies between 1993 and 2005. On the other hand, fictional Ranger Woodrow Call has been portrayed by four different actors: Tommy Lee Jones in *Lonesome Dove* (1989), Jon Voight in *Return to Lonesome Dove* (1993), James Garner in *Streets of Laredo* (1995), and Johnny Lee Miller in *Dead Man's Walk* (1996).

Problems sometimes arise when actors portray real-life Rangers. Aside from the Hamer lawsuit, historians complained that Dylan McDermott's performance as Captain Leander McNelly in *Texas Rangers* (2001) strayed too far from fact—including a fictional scene wherein Rangers kill gunman John Fisher, and another that shows McNelly dying before his retirement. In *The Town That Dreaded Sundown* (1976), director Charles Pierce renamed Lone Wolf Gonzaullas as "J.D. Morales" and fabricated a near-miss shootout with Texarkana's "Moonlight Murderer" that never occurred in real life—but which left the still-unknown killer limping on-screen.

RIDING ON AIR

Lone Star lawmen captured America's airwaves in the mid-1930s, when Kellogg's cereal sponsored *Riding with the Texas Rangers,* and returned on July 8, 1950, when NBC Radio aired its first episode of *Tales of the Texas Rangers.* Film star Joel McCrea portrayed Ranger Jace Pearson, riding his trusty horse Charcoal in pursuit of outlaws and rustlers, while using the latest scientific crime-fighting techniques. The program aired 95 half-hour episodes between its premiere and its final broadcast on September 14, 1952. Actor Stacy Keach Sr. (1914–2003) directed the programs, which were produced by Screen Gems and sponsored by Wheaties cereal. Keach received technical advice from real-life Ranger Captain Manuel "Lone Wolf" Gonzaullas.[9]

TV RANGERS

Television was the last frontier conquered by Texas Rangers. First on the small screen was *The Lone Ranger,* a popular series airing from September 1949 through June 1957. *Tales of the Texas Rangers* jumped from radio to TV in August 1955, airing 52 episodes on

TEX WILLER

Any doubt of the Texas Rangers' international appeal was banished in September 1948, with the appearance of the first "Tex Willer" comic book in Italy. The title character fights crime in the Old West with fellow Ranger Kit Carson. (The historical Kit Carson [1809–1868] was not a Ranger, though he fought in some of Texas's Indian wars and played a small role in the Mexican War.) Produced over time by 11 authors and 37 illustrators, Tex Willer rode far beyond the confines of Texas, truly conquering the world.[10]

Born in the years after World War II crushed Italy's cruel fascist dictatorship, Tex Willer emerged as an enemy of prejudice and injustice, married to a beautiful Navajo named Lilith and aided by her tribe in his adventures. His other allies include a Canadian Mounty, Apache chief Cochise, a reformed outlaw serving as vice president of Mexico, and an Egyptian wizard named El Morisco. Aside from common outlaws, his enemies include a collection of warlocks and mad scientists (Mefisto, Maestro, etc.), a human chameleon called Proteus, and the Black Tiger (an evil prince from Borneo).

That cast of characters may explain the global appeal of Tex Willis, still in print and going strong more than 60 years after his debut. Argentina saw his exploits published in the magazine *Rayo Rojo,* in the 1950s. Finland ran the stories from 1953–1965, then took a five-year hiatus before resuming publication. Yugoslavians enjoyed the comics from the 1960s until their country broke up in 1989. Since 1971, the comics have been more or less continuously published in Brazil, Finland, India, and Israel, with no sign of declining popularity. Serbia, once part of Yugoslavia, resumed publication in 2008.[11]

CBS before its cancellation in December 1958. Willard Parker and Harry Lauter starred as Rangers Jace Pearson and Clay Morgan, with an unusual twist. Some episodes found the Rangers chasing outlaws from the 19th century, while others had the same two lawmen solving modern-day crimes, driving a truck with a horse trailer attached. Despite the apparent time travel, one message always came through: "They'll fight for Right, for Right and Justice, to Enforce the Law for You!"[12]

Director Sam Peckinpah (1925–1984)—best known for his films *Ride the High Country* (1962), *The Wild Bunch* (1969) and *Straw Dogs* (1971)—preceded those Hollywood hits with *Trackdown,* a TV series starring Robert Culp as Texas Ranger Hoby Gilman. Seventy episodes aired on CBS between the series premiere in October 1957 and its closure in September 1959.[13] A March 1958 episode featured Steve McQueen as bounty hunter Josh Randall, launching McQueen's new Western series *Wanted: Dead or Alive* in September 1958. Robert Culp, in turn, went on to star with Bill Cosby in the popular *I Spy* series during 1965–1968.

The next Ranger television series was *Laredo,* which premiered in September 1965 and aired 56 episodes before ending its run in April 1967. The characters—including Captain Ed Parmalee (Philip Caree) and three mismatched Rangers, Reese Bennett (Neville Brand), Chad Cooper (Peter Brown), and Joe Riley (William Smith)—first appeared in an episode of *The Virginian,* aired by NBC in April 1965, later released theatrically as *Backtrack* (1969). Set on the 19th-century frontier, *Laredo* followed its cast in pursuit of renegades and outlaws, often with a comic twist. Three episodes from the show's first season were combined in 1968 to create the feature film *Three Guns for Texas.*[14]

The latest Texas Ranger to secure a long-term TV audience is Captain Cordell Walker, portrayed by Chuck Norris. The *Walker, Texas Ranger* series premiered on the USA network in April 1993 and ran through 196 episodes before its two-part "Final Showdown" aired in May 2001. *Walker* brought diversity to the force, with Clarence Gilyard Jr. portraying African-American Ranger James Trivette, and spawned three full-length TV movies including *Walker, Texas Ranger* (1993), *Walker, Texas Ranger: Deadly Reunion* (1994), and *Walker, Texas Ranger: Trial By Fire* (2005). Curiously, Cordell Walker seems to be the only Ranger on record who wears a black hat.[15]

Chuck Norris played the title character in the TV series *Walker, Texas Ranger* from 1993 to 2001. (*Corbis Sygma*)

A HOUSEHOLD NAME

No law enforcement agency on Earth can match the Texas Rangers when it comes to recognition as a household word. If imitation is, indeed, the most sincere form of flattery, then Texas Rangers must feel flattered by adoption of the "Ranger" label by police in other states, including

- California, where Governor John Bigler created the California State Rangers—led by former Texas Ranger Captain Harry Love—to hunt down bandit Joaquin Murrieta's gang in May 1853. The Rangers killed Murrieta two months later, then disbanded, although some folktales claim they shot the wrong man. Harry Love lived on to create the California State Police in 1887.
- Colorado, where the Jefferson Rangers organized as the first state-wide police force in 1859. Renamed the Colorado Rangers in 1861, the unit remained in service until Governor William Sweet disbanded it in January 1923.
- Arizona, where the first state police force—dubbed Arizona Rangers—was formed in 1901, openly borrowing its structure and methods from the Texas Rangers. Dissolved by law in 1909, the Arizona Rangers were reformed in 1957.
- New Mexico, where state lawmakers created the New Mexico Mounted Police in 1905. Despite its formal name, the unit was commonly called Fullerton's Rangers, in honor of its first commander, Captain John Fullerton. The force disbanded in February 1921.

Texas Rangers have also left their mark on professional sports, beginning with the New York Rangers hockey team, created in 1926. One of the oldest teams in the National Hockey League, the New York Rangers were the first American NHL team to win the Stanley Cup (in 1928), and have repeated that victory on three occasions (in 1933, 1940 and 1994). Another pro hockey team, the Colorado Rangers (renamed from the Indianapolis Checkers in 1987), changed its name to the Denver Rangers in 1988.

Meanwhile, the Washington Senators baseball team moved from the nation's capital to Dallas, Texas, in 1972 and changed its name to the Texas Rangers. By 2008, the Rangers had won 3,570 games and lost 4,059. Since 1994, when Rangers Ballpark opened in the Dallas suburb of Arlington, the team has placed first in the Western Division of the American League five times, but it remains the only franchise that has never won a playoff series in American League history. It joins the Seattle Mariners and Washington Nationals as one of three Major League Baseball teams that have never played in a World Series.[16]

Sports teams aside, the Texas Rangers name—and the much broader concept of "ranging"—has been used to market all manner of commercial products, from food to motor vehicles and aircraft. While sponsoring its *Riding with the Texas Rangers* radio show in the mid-1930s, the Kellogg Company created a promotional club called the Junior Texas Rangers, open to children who mailed in cereal box tops. Each member received a "commission," a badge, and the opportunity to buy Junior Texas Ranger hats, clothing, rings, and toy pistols. Twenty years later, beginning in the 1950s and continuing through the 1960s, Texas Ranger and Rangerette bicycles lured young riders. Today, they are collectible antiques. Adult consumers also heard the call of Ranger marketing, from manufacturers of Texas Ranger Motor Oil in the 1950s.

Today, staff members at the Texas Ranger Research Center credit Lone Star lawmen for inspiring any product that bears the "Ranger" name, including Bell/Ranger outdoor apparel, marketed for hunters since 1957; various helicopters introduced by Fort Worth's Bell Helicopter Textron firm since 1962, including the Model 47J Ranger, the 206L LongRanger, the Bell 400 TwinRanger, the TH-57 Sea Ranger, and the Bell 206 JetRanger; and Ford Ranger pickup trucks, manufactured since 1965.[17] While some of those claims may strain the imagination, there is no doubt concerning Bell's 206L Texas Ranger (a military helicopter introduced in 1981), or the line of Winchester Ranger Law Enforcement ammunition sold only to police departments (advertised with a badge resembling that of the early Texas Rangers).[18]

For the would-be Rangers with a sweet tooth, there are even Texas Ranger cookies—and their recipes, as published on the Internet, reveal as many variations as the real-life frontier lawmen who inspired them.[19]

Chronology

1823	Stephen Austin creates two Ranger companies for "common defense"
1835	Anglo settlers rebel against the Mexican government
1836	**March 6:** Members of the Gonzales Ranging Company die defending the Alamo
1837	**March:** Washington recognizes the Republic of Texas
1844	**January 23:** Law passed authorizing Jack Hays to raise a Ranger company
	June 1: Hays and 14 Rangers battle Comanches at Walker's Creek
1845	**December 29:** Texas becomes the 28th American state
1846	**May 13:** The United States declares war on Mexico
1848	**February 2:** Treaty of Guadalupe Hidalgo ends the Mexican War, establishing the Rio Grande as the southern border of Texas
1859	**December 27:** Rangers defeat Mexican bandit Juan Cortina's gang at Rio Grande City
1861	**February 1:** Texas secedes from the Union, joining the Confederacy on March 2
1865	**April 9:** Confederate Army surrenders in Virginia
1870	**March 30:** Texas readmitted to the Union
1874	**April 10:** New legislation authorizes 450 Rangers for frontier defense
1877	**December 12:** Rangers intervene in the El Paso Salt War
1901	**March 29:** Texas Rangers downsized to four companies of state police

1910	**April 9:** Release date of *The Ranger's Bride,* first movie about Texas Rangers
1917	**April 6:** The United States enters World War I **May:** Ranger Home Guard Act authorizes hiring of 1,000 officers
1918	**January 28:** Rangers execute 15 Mexican civilians in the Porvenir Massacre, prompting disbandment of Company B on June 4
1920	**January 16:** Eighteenth Amendment bans liquor nationwide
1925	**January 20:** Miriam Ferguson begins first term as governor of Texas
1933	**January 17:** Miriam Ferguson resumes office as governor; 40 Rangers resign while the rest are replaced with political cronies **December 5:** Twenty-first Amendment repeals Prohibition
1935	**August 10:** Texas Department of Public Safety created with Texas Rangers as one of six division
1941	**December 8:** America enters World War II; Texas Rangers assume civil defense duties
1968	Texas Rangers Museum opens in Waco
1976	Texas Ranger Hall of Fame established at Texas Rangers Museum in Waco
1993	**August:** Texas Rangers hire first two female officers
1994	Ranger Cheryl Steadman resigns, claiming sexual discrimination
1997	**April 27 to May 3:** "Republic of Texas" siege in Jeff Davis County
1999	**July 13:** Ranger Drew Carter arrests serial killer Angel Maturino Resindiz
2003	Trooper Juanita Alvarado sues the Rangers for rejecting her application five times
2007	**July 16:** Juanita Alvarado loses her lawsuit against the Rangers
2008	**April 3:** Rangers join in raid on polygamist YFZ Ranch near Eldorado

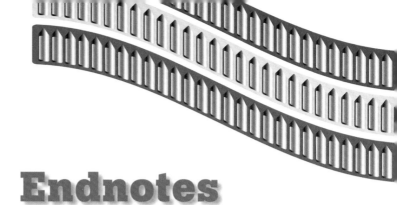

Endnotes

Introduction

1. John Weems, "Galveston Hurricane of 1900," *Handbook of Texas Online,* http://www. tshaonline. org/handbook/online/articles/ GG/ydg2.html (Accessed May 29, 2010).

2. Officer Down Memorial Page, http://www.odmp.org/ agency/3825-texas-department-of-public-safety---texas-rangers-texas (Accessed May 29, 2010).

3. Texas Ranger Research Center, http://www.texasranger.org/ ReCenter/RCenter.htm (Accessed May 29, 2010).

Chapter 1

1. "Moses Austin," *Handbook of Texas Online,* http://www.tsha online.org/handbook/online/ articles/AA/fau12.html (Accessed May 29, 2010).

2. Mike Cox, "A Brief History of the Texas Rangers," http://www.texas ranger.org/history/BriefHistory1. htm (Accessed May 29, 2010).

3. Ibid.

4. "Stephen Fuller Austin," *Handbook of Texas Online,* http://www. tshaonline.org/handbook/online/ articles/AA/fau14.html (Accessed May 29, 2010).

5. Allen Hatley, "Sam Walker," *Texas Ranger Dispatch Magazine,* http://

www.texasranger.org/dispatch/ Backissues/Dispatch_Issue_02.pdf (Accessed June 29, 2010).

6. "Battle of Walker's Creek," *Handbook of Texas Online,* http://www. tshaonline.org/handbook/online/ articles/WW/btw2.html (Accessed May 29, 2010).

7. Ibid.

8. "The Mexican War," http://www. lone-star.net/mall/texasinfo/mexi cow.htm (Accessed May 29, 2010).

Chapter 2

1. Officer Down Memorial Page, http://www.odmp.org/ officer/19666-private-d.-c.-(doc)-sullivan (Accessed May 29, 2010).

2. "Mexican War," http://www. globalsecurity.org/military/ops/ mexican_war.htm (Accessed May 29, 2010).

3. Ibid.

4. Robert Leckie, *From Sea to Shining Sea* (New York: HarperPerennial, 1993), 545.

5. Leckie, 545; "The Texas Rangers: From Horses to Helicopters," *Texas Almanac,* http://www.texasalma nac.com/history/highlights/ rangers (Accessed May 29, 2010).

6. Ibid.

7. Texas Ranger Research Center, http://www.texasranger.org/ ReCenter/killedlist.htm#military

(Accessed May 29, 2010); List of 1846-48; U.S. Army Casualties, http://www.dmwv.org/honoring/other.htm (Accessed May 29, 2010).

8. Richard Griswold del Castillo, "War's End: Treaty of Guadalupe Hidalgo," http://www.pbs.org/kera/usmexicanwar/war/wars_end_guadalupe.html (Accessed May 29, 2010).

9. Charles Robinson III, *The Men Who Wear the Star* (New York: Random House, 2000), 105.

10. "The Texas Rangers: From Horses to Helicopters," *Texas Almanac,* http://www. texasalmanac. com/history/highlights/rangers (Accessed May 29, 2010).

11. Texas Ranger Hall of Fame, http://www.texasranger.org/halloffame/Ford_John.htm (Accessed May 29, 2010).

12. Robinson, 114–115.

13. Jerry Denson, "The Battle of Little Robe Creek, 1858" Ellis County Historical Society, http://www.usgennet.org/usa/ok/county/ellis/littlerobe.html (Accessed May 29, 2010).

14. "John Coffee Hays," *Handbook of Texas Online,* http://www.tshaonline.org/handbook/online/articles/HH/fhabq.html (Accessed May 29, 2010).

15. "Juan Nepomuceno Cortina," *Handbook of Texas Online,* http://www.tshaonline.org/handbook/online/articles/CC/fco73.html (Accessed May 29, 2010).

16. Bill O'Neal, "Captain Jack Hays," *Texas Ranger Dispatch Magazine,* http://www.texasranger.org/dispatch/Backissues/Dispatch_Issue_01.pdf (Accessed June 29, 2010).

17. Ibid.

18. "Juan Nepomuceno Cortina."

19. "William A.A. Wallace," Texas Ranger Hall of Fame, http://www.texasranger.org/ halloffame/Wallace_William.htm (Accessed May 29, 2010).

20. Steve Moore, "William A.A. 'Bigfoot' Wallace," *Texas Ranger Dispatch Magazine,* http://www.texasranger.org/dispatch/Back issues/Dispatch_Issue_12.pdf (Accessed June 29, 2010).

21. "Cynthia Ann Parker," http://www.spartacus.schoolnet.co.uk/WWparkerCA.htm (Accessed May 29, 2010); "Cynthia Ann Parker," *Handbook of Texas Online,* http://www.tshaonline.org/handbook/online/articles/PP/fpa18.html (Accessed May 29, 2010).

22. Ibid.

23. Texas Ranger History, http://www.texasranger.org/history/Timedefend.htm (Accessed May 29, 2010).

24. Allen Trelease, *White Terror* (New York: Harper & Row, 1971), 103–104.

25. Robert Utley, "Forgotten Rangers," *Texas Ranger Dispatch Magazine,* http://www.texasranger.org/dispatch/Backissues/Dispatch_Issue_01.pdf (Accessed June 29, 2010); Trelease, 148.

26. Lyle Brown, Joyce Langenegger and Sonia Garcia, *Practicing Texas Politics* (Boston: Houghton Mifflin, 2006), 67–68.

Chapter 3

1. "John B. Jones," *Handbook of Texas Online,* http://www.tshaonline.org/handbook/online/articles/JJ/fjo54.html (Accessed May 29, 2010).

2. Texas Legends: The Sutton-Taylor Feud of DeWitt County, http://www. legendsofamerica.com/

tx-suttontaylor.html (Accessed
May 29, 2010).

3. "John B. Jones," *Handbook of
Texas Online.*

4. "Mason County War," *Handbook of
Texas Online,* http://www.tsha
online.org/handbook/online/
articles/MM/jcm1.html (Accessed
May 29, 2010).

5. "Leander H. McNelly," *Handbook
of Texas Online,* http://www.tsha
online.org/handbook/online/
articles/MM/fmcag.html
(Accessed May 29, 2010).

6. "Horrell-Higgins Feud," *Handbook of Texas Online,* http://www.
tshaonline.org/handbook/online/
articles/HH/jch3.html (Accessed
May 29, 2010).

7. "John King Fisher," *Handbook of
Texas Online,* http://www.tshaon
line.org/handbook/online/articles/
FF/ffi20.html (Accessed May 29,
2010); John King Fisher, http://www.
ccchaney.com/Damron/king
fisher.html (Accessed May 29, 2010).

8. Eugene Cunningham, *Triggernom-
etry* (Norman, Okla.: University of
Oklahoma Press, 1996), 38–65; Bill
O'Neal, *The Pimlico Encyclopedia
of Western Gunfighters* (London:
Pimlico, 1998), 4–5, 126–131.

9. "Fence Cutting," *Handbook of Texas
Online,* http://www.tshaonline.org/
handbook/online/articles/FF/auf1.
html (Accessed May 29, 2010).

10. Cox, http://www.texasranger.
org/history/BriefHistory1.htm
(Accessed May 29, 2010).

11. Ibid.

12. "Laredo Smallpox Riot," *Handbook of Texas Online,* http://www.
tshaonline.org/handbook/online/
articles/LL/jcl1.html (Accessed
May 29, 2010).

13. "Galveston Hurricane of 1900,"
Handbook of Texas Online, http://

www.tshaonline. org/handbook/
online/articles/GG/ydg2.html
(Accessed May 29, 2010).

14. "Frontier Battalion," *Handbook of
Texas Online,* http://www.tsha
online.org/handbook/online/
articles/FF/qqf1.html (Accessed
May 29, 2010).

Chapter 4

1. Ruth Spence, *Nickel Plated Highway to Hell* (McAllen, Texas: n.p.,
1989), 28-29.

2. Spence, 29-30; Officer Down
Memorial Page, http://www.odmp.
org/officer/18393-private-w.-emm
ett-robuck (Accessed May 29,
2010).

3. Cox, "Texas Ranger History,"
http://www.texasranger.org/history
/BriefHistory1.htm (Accessed May
29, 2010).

4. Officer Down Memorial Page,
http://www.odmp.org/agency/
4777-texas-rangers-texas
(Accessed May 29, 2010).

5. "William Jesse McDonald,"
Handbook of Texas Online, http://
www.tshaonline.org/handbook/
online/articles/MM/fmc43.html
(Accessed May 29, 2010).

6. Benjamin Johnson, *Revolution in
Texas* (New Haven, Conn.: Yale
University Press, 2005), 71–143.

7. "Plan of San Diego," *Handbook of
Texas Online,* http://www.tsha
online.org/handbook/online/
articles/PP/ngp4.html (Accessed
May 29, 2010).

8. "Texas Rangers," *Handbook of
Texas Online,* http://www.tshaon-
line.org/handbook/online/articles/
TT/met4.html (Accessed May 29,
2010).

9. "Brite Ranch Raid," *Handbook of
Texas Online,* http://www.tsha
online.org/handbook/online/

articles/BB/qyb2.html (Accessed May 29, 2010).

10. "Porvenir Massacre," *Handbook of Texas Online,* http://www.tsha online.org/handbook/online/ articles/PP/jcp2.html (Accessed May 29, 2010).

11. Ibid.

12. Ibid.

13. "The Zimmermann Telegram," National Archives, http://www. archives.gov/education/lessons/zim-mermann (Accessed May 29, 2010).

14. "Texas Rangers," *Handbook of Texas Online.*

15. Chronology of the American Brewing Industry, http://www. beerhistory.com/library/holdings/ chronology.shtml (Accessed May 29, 2010).

16. Kathleen Drowne, *Spirits of Defi-ance* (Columbus: Ohio State University Press, 2006), 35–36.

17. William Helmer and Rick Mattix, *Public Enemies* (New York: Check-mark, 1998), 65; Cox, "Texas Ranger History"; Officer Down Memorial Page, http://www.odmp. org/officer/14194-special-ranger-timothy-samuel-willard (Accessed May 29, 2010).

18. "Dry Counties," Texas State Direc-tory, http://www.txdirectory.com/ online/county/? page=1&dry=1 (Accessed May 29, 2010).

19. "Martial Law Grips Texas Oil Cen-tre," *New York Times,* January 13, 1922.

20. "Texas Rangers: From Horses to Helicopters," Texas Almanac, http://www.texasalmanac.com/ history/ highlights/rangers (Accessed May 29, 2010).

21. Cox, "Texas Ranger History."

22. Charles Alexander, *The Ku Klux Klan in the Southwest* (Norman, Okla.: University of Oklahoma Press, 1995), 192; David Chalmers, *Hooded Americanism* (Durham, N.C.: Duke University Press, 1981), 42, 45.

23. "Miriam Amanda Wallace Fergu-son," *Handbook of Texas Online,* http://www.tshaonline.org/hand book/online/articles/FF/ffe6.html (Accessed May 29, 2010).

24. "Great Depression," *Handbook of Texas Online,* http://www.tsha online.org/handbook/online/ articles/GG/npg1.html (Accessed May 29, 2010).

25. Helmer and Mattix, 144.

26. Joseph Geringer, "Bonnie & Clyde: Romeo and Juliet in a Get-away Car," Crime Library, http:// www.trutv.com/library/crime/ gangsters_outlaws/outlaws/bon-nie/1.html (Accessed May 29, 2010).

Chapter 5

1. "Starr County Strike," *Handbook of Texas Online,* http://www.tsha online.org/handbook/online/ articles/SS/oes3.html (Accessed May 29, 2010).

2 "Alfred Young Allee," *Handbook of Texas Online,* http://www.tsha online.org/handbook/online/ articles/AA/fal97.html (Accessed May 29, 2010); *Allee v. Medrano,* 416 U.S. 802 (1974).

3. "Texas Rangers," *Handbook of Texas Online.*

4. "Texas Rangers," *Handbook of Texas Online*; "Texas Rangers," *Texas Almanac.*

5. Cox, "Texas Ranger History"; "Texas Rangers," *Handbook of Texas Online*; "Homer Garrison Jr.," *Handbook of Texas Online,* http://www.tshaonline.org/hand-book/online/articles/GG/fga34. html (Accessed May 29, 2010).

6. Texas Ranger History, http://www. texasranger.org/history/Timespecial.htm (Accessed May 29, 2010).

7. "German Prisoners of War," *Handbook of Texas Online,* http://www. tshaonline.org/handbook/online/ articles/GG/qug1.html (Accessed May 29, 2010).

8. "Rusk State Hospital," *Handbook of Texas Online,* http://www.tsha online.org/handbook/online/ articles/RR/sbr3.html (Accessed May 29, 2010).

9. "Texas Rangers," *Handbook of Texas Online*; Cox, "Texas Ranger History."

10. Vanessa Jackson, "An Early History–African American Mental Health," http://academic.udayton. edu/health/01status/mental01.htm (Accessed May 29, 2010).

11. "Rusk State Hospital," *Handbook of Texas Online.*

12. "Mansfield School Desegregation Incident," *Handbook of Texas Online,* http://www.tshaonline.org/ handbook/online/articles/MM/ jcm2.html (Accessed May 29, 2010).

13. "Urbanization," *Handbook of Texas Online,* http://www.tshaonline. org/handbook/online/articles/UU/ hyunw.html (Accessed May 29, 2010).

14. Robert Nieman, "Galveston's Balinese Room," *Texas Ranger Dispatch Magazine,* http://www.texasranger.org/dispatch/Backissues/ Dispatch_Issue_27.pdf (Accessed June 29, 2010).

15. Ibid.

16. Ibid.

17. Ibid.

18. "Texas Rangers," *Handbook of Texas Online.*

19. "Alfred Young Allee," *Handbook of Texas Online.*

20. "Crystal City Revolts," *Handbook of Texas Online,* http://www. tshaonline.org/handbook/online/ articles/CC/wmc1.html (Accessed May 29, 2010).

21. Dwight Watson, Race and the Houston Police Department, 1930-1990 (College Station, Texas: Texas A&M University Press, 2006), 77–86; Mario Salas, "Veteran of the Civil Rights Movement Turns 90 This Year," African-American News & Issues, http://www.aframnews.com/html/2006-09-13/lead3. htm (Accessed May 29, 2010).

22. "Homer Garrison Jr.," *Handbook of Texas Online.*

23. "Texas Rangers," *Handbook of Texas Online.*

24. "Texas Ranger Hall of Fame and Museum," *Handbook of Texas Online,* http://www. tshaonline.org/ handbook/online/articles/TT /lbt3.html (Accessed May 29, 2010).

Chapter 6

1. Texas Ranger History, http://www. texasranger.org/history/HKidnapp ping.htm (Accessed May 29, 2010).

2. Ibid.

3. Wilson Speir, http://www.cemetery .state.tx.us/pub/user_form.asp? step=1&pers_id =2736 (Accessed May 29, 2010).

4. Mike Cox, "Barbecue Bust," http://www.texasescapes.com/ MikeCox TexasTales/164Barbe cueBust.htm (Accessed May 29, 2010).

5. "Texas Rangers," *Handbook of Texas Online.*

6. Texas Ranger History, http://www. texasranger.org/history/cases.htm (Accessed May 29, 2010).

7. Texas Ranger Hall of Fame, http:// www.texasranger.org/halloffame/

Doherty_Bobby.htm; Officer Down Memorial Page, http://www.odmp.org/officer/4152-ranger-bobby-paul-doherty (Accessed May 29, 2010).

8. Mike Cox, "Texas Ranger History," http://www.texasranger.org/history/BriefHistory2. htm (Accessed May 29, 2010).

9. Texas Ranger History, http://www.texasranger.org/history/cases.htm (Accessed May 29, 2010).

10. Texas Ranger Research Center, http://www.texasranger.org/ReCenter/hispanic_ indian_rangers.htm (Accessed May 29, 2010); Texas Ranger Hall of Fame, http://www.texasranger.org/visitor/FAQ.htm (Accessed May 29, 2010); "Texas Rangers," *Texas Almanac*; Sam Verhovek, "Women Rangers: Struggle in a macho bastion," *New York Times*, August 27, 1995.

11. "Texas Rangers," *Texas Almanac*; Texas Ranger Hall of Fame, http://www.texasranger.org/visitor/FAQ. htm (Accessed May 29, 2010).

12. Verhovek; "Texas Rangers open sexual harassment hearings; recalls case involving black female sergeant," *Jet*, http://findarticles.com/p/articles/mi_m1355/is_ n12_v88/ai_ 17361556 (Accessed May 29, 2010); "State agency rules Rangers didn't harass female member," *Victoria* (Texas) *Advocate*, January 17, 1996.

13. Texas Ranger Research Center, http://www.texasranger.org/ReCenter/hispanic_ indian_rangers.htm (Accessed May 29, 2010); "Texas Rangers diversifying," *New York Times*, June 24, 1993.

14. "Texas Rangers," *Handbook of Texas Online*.

15. "Texas Rangers," *Texas Almanac*.

16. "Texas Rangers," *Handbook of Texas Online*; "Texas Rangers," *Texas Almanac*.

17. Robert Nieman, "Matt Cawthon," *Texas Ranger Dispatch Magazine*, http://www.texasranger.org/dispatch/Backissues/Dispatch_Issue_15.pdf (Accessed May 29, 2010).

18. Ibid.

19. Joseph Geringer, "Angel Maturino Resendez: The Railroad Killer," http://www.trutv. com/library/crime/serial_killers/notorious/resendez/track_1.html (Accessed May 29, 2010).

20. Republic of Texas, http://texasrepublic.info/index.html (Accessed May 29, 2010).

21. Texas Ranger History, http://www.texasranger.org/history/Timespe cial.htm (Accessed May 29, 2010).

22. "'Middle Man' Who Forwarded Bribe Payments to Willacy County Commissioners Sentenced," U.S. Federal News Service (November 21, 2006), http://www.highbeam.com/doc/1P3-1191894491.html (Accessed May 29, 2010).

23. Barbara Ramirez and Beth Wilson, "Smith denies sex assault; Texas Rangers investigate," *Corpus Christi Caller-Times*, April 24, 2007; "Smith to be reassigned Jan. 5," *Corpus Christi Caller-Times*, December 20, 2008.

24. Texas Attorney General's Office, August 7, 2007; U.S. Department of Justice, March 13, 2008.

25. "Drug busts continue," *Clear Creek* (Texas) *Pilot*, February 5, 2008.

26. "False abuse claim investigated in Texas polygamist raid," KEYE-TV, Channel 42 (Austin, Texas), April 20, 2008.

27. "Texas Rangers investigate officer-involved shooting in Electra,"

Wichita Falls (Texas) *Times Record News,* May 19, 2008.

28. Joey Dauben, "Clerk under Texas Rangers investigation," *Ellis County Press,* December 1, 2008.

29. "TABC and Texas Rangers Investigate Aggravated Assault at Underage Drinking Party," Texas Alcoholic Beverage Commission (December 23, 2008), http://www.tabc.state.tx.us/home/press_releases/2008/20081223.asp (Accessed May 29, 2010).

30. "Rangers Investigate Incident Involving Former Central Texas Officer," KWTX-TV, Channel 10 (Waco, Texas), March 16, 2009.

31. "Inmate death under investigation," KGNS-TV, Channel 8 (Laredo, Texas), April 29, 2009; "Deputy arrested for theft," KGNS-TV, Channel 8, May 1, 2009.

32. Scott Goldstein, "Texas Department of Public Safety director resigns following sexual harassment allegations," *Dallas Morning News,* May 5, 2009.

33. "Texas Rangers," *Texas Almanac.*

34. Texas Ranger Hall of Fame and Museum, http://www.texasranger.org/today/rangerstoday.htm (Accessed May 29, 2010).

Chapter 7

1. Chuck Parsons, "The Border Boss: John R. Hughes," *Texas Rangers Dispatch Magazine*, http://www.texasranger.org/dispatch/Backissues/Dispatch_Issue_10.pdf (Accessed May 29, 2010).

2. Officer Down Memorial Page, http://www.odmp.org/agency/3825-texas-department-of-public-safety---texas-rangers-texas (Accessed May 29, 2010).

3. Frederick Wilkins, *The Law Comes to Texas* (Austin: State House Press, 1999), 227.

4. S&W Forum, http://smith-wesson forum.com/ (Accessed May 29, 2010).

5. Robert Nieman, "Frank Hamer," *Texas Ranger Dispatch Magazine,* http://www.texasranger.org/dispatch/Backissues/Dispatch_Issue_11.pdf (Accessed June 29, 2010).

6. S&W Forum.

7. Nieman.

8. Texas Ranger Hall of Fame, http://www.texasranger.org/halloffame/McDonald_Jesse.htm (Accessed May 29, 2010).

9. Texas Ranger Hall of Fame, http://www.texasranger.org/halloffame/Hughes_John.htm (Accessed May 29, 2010).

10. "John Reynolds Hughes," *Handbook of Texas Online,* http://www.tshaonline.org/handbook/online/articles/HH/fhu18.html (Accessed June 30, 2010).

11. "Manuel Trazazas Gonzaullas," *Handbook of Texas Online,* http://www.tshaonline. org/handbook/online/articles/GG/fgo38.html (Accessed May 29, 2010).

12. "Jaybird-Woodpecker War," *Handbook of Texas Online,* http://www.tshaonline.org/handbook/online/articles/JJ/wfj1.html (Accessed May 29, 2010).

13. Robert Nieman, "They Just Passed the Bucket," *Texas Ranger Dispatch Magazine,* http://www.texasranger.org/dispatch/Backissues/Dispatch_Issue_03.pdf (Accessed June 29, 2010).

14. "Ira Aten," *Handbook of Texas Online,* http://www.tshaonline.org/handbook/ online/articles/AA/

fat9_print.html (Accessed May 29, 2010).

15. "John Harris Rogers," *Handbook of Texas Online,* http://www.tshaon line.org/handbook/online/articles/ RR/frojb.html (Accessed May 29, 2010).

16. Robert Nieman, "Bob Goss," *Texas Ranger Dispatch Magazine,* http://www.texasranger.org/dispatch/ Backissues/Dispatch_Issue_16.pdf (Accessed May 29, 2010).

17. Ibid.

Chapter 8

1. Merriam-Webster Online, http://www.merriam-webster.com/span ish/tonto (Accessed May 29, 2010).

2. Lone Ranger Fan Club, http://www.lonerangerfanclub.com/index.html (Accessed May 29, 2010).

3. "The Lone Ranger," Internet Movie Database.

4. "The Lone Ranger," Internet Movie Database; Texas Rangers Research Center.

5. "The Lone Ranger," Internet Movie Database; Lone Ranger Fan Club.

6. Pulp Rack, http://pulprack.com/ arch/2002/09/texas_rangers_m. html (Accessed May 29, 2010).

7. Ibid.

8. Texas Ranger Research Center, http://www.texasranger.org/ ReCenter/movies.htm (Accessed May 29, 2010).

9. "Tales of the Texas Rangers," http://www.oldtimeradio fans.com/template.php?show_ name=Tales%20Of%20The%20 Texas%20Rangers (Accessed May 29, 2010).

10. "Tex FAQ," http://www.ubcfumetti. com/tx/faq_en.htm (Accessed May 29, 2010).

11. "Tex FAQ."

12. "Tales of the Texas Rangers," Internet Movie Database, http://www.imdb.com/title/tt0047781 (Accessed May 29, 2010).

13. "Trackdown," Internet Movie Database, http://www.imdb.com/ title/tt0050071 (Accessed May 29, 2010).

14. "Laredo," Internet Movie Database, http://www.imdb.com/title/ tt0058819 (Accessed May 29, 2010).

15. "Walker, Texas Ranger," Internet Movie Database, http://www.imdb. com/title/tt0106168 (Accessed on May 29, 2010); Texas Ranger Research Center.

16. "Texas Rangers," SportsEcyclope-dia, http://www.sportsecyclopedia. com/al/texas/texrangers.html (Accessed June 29, 2010).

17. Texas Rangers Research Center.

18. Winchester Ammunition, http://www.winchester.com/Products/le/ Pages/default.aspx (Accessed May 29, 2010).

19. BigOven, http://www.bigoven. com/28690-Texas-Ranger-Cookies-recipe.html (Accessed May 29, 2010); Cooks.com, http://www.cooks.com/rec/search/0,1-91,ranger_cookies,FF.html (Accessed May 29, 2010); Sleepy Cat Hollow, http://sleepycathollow. wordpress.com/2009/03/13/texas-ranger-cookie-recipe-frontier-chuckwagon-cookin (Accessed May 29, 2010); Chef2Chef, http://recipes.chef2chef.net/ recipe-archive/10/062661.shtml (Accessed May 29, 2010).

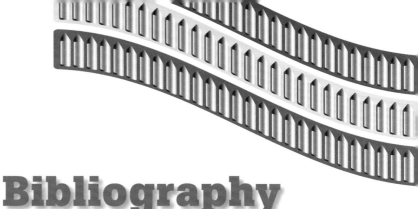

Bibliography

Cox, Mike. *The Texas Rangers: Wearing the Cinco Peso, 1821–1900*. New York: Macmillan, 2008.

Davis, John. *The Texas Rangers: Their First 150 Years*. San Antonio: University of Texas Institute of Texan Cultures, 1992.

Harris, Charles, and Louis Sadler. *The Texas Rangers and the Mexican Revolution: The Bloodiest Decade, 1910–1920*. Albuquerque: University of New Mexico Press, 2004.

Robinson, Charles. *The Men Who Wear the Star: The Story of the Texas Rangers*. New York: Random House, 2000.

Utley, Robert. *Lone Star Justice: The First Century of the Texas Rangers*. New York: Oxford University Press, 2002.

———. *Lone Star Lawmen: The Second Century of the Texas Rangers*. New York: Oxford University Press, 2007.

Webb, Walter. *The Texas Rangers: A Century of Frontier Defense*. Austin: University of Texas Press, 1989.

Wilkins, Frederick. *The Law Comes to Texas: The Texas Rangers 1870–1901*. Abilene, Texas: State House Press, 1999.

———. *The Legend Begins: The Texas Rangers, 1823-1845*. Abilene, Texas: State House Press, 1996.

Further Resources

Print

Malsch, Brownson. *"Lone Wolf" Gonzaullas, Texas Ranger*. Norman, Okla.: University of Oklahoma Press, 1998. Biography of a famous Ranger captain.

Procter, Ben. *Just One Riot: Episodes of Texas Rangers in the 20th Century*. Waco, Texas: Eakin Press, 2000. A history of Ranger cases from the 20th century.

Samora, Julian, Joe Bernal, and Albert Peña. *Gunpowder Justice: A Reassessment of the Texas Rangers*. Notre Dame, Ind.: University of Notre Dame Press, 1979. A critical view of Ranger conflict with Mexicans and Hispanic Americans.

Online

Texas Department of Public Safety
http://www.txdps.state.tx.us/index.htm
Information on all aspects of the department's operations.

Texas Ranger Hall of Fame and Museum
http://www.texasranger.org
Comprehensive coverage of the Rangers throughout history.

Texas Rangers Law Enforcement Association
http://www.texasrangers.org
Nonprofit organization created to promote appreciation of the Rangers.

Index

123

About the Author

Michael Newton has published 229 books since 1977, with 18 forthcoming from various houses through 2011. His history of the Florida Ku Klux Klan (*The Invisible Empire*, 2001) won the Florida Historical Society's 2002 Rembert Patrick Award for "Best Book in Florida History," and his *Encyclopedia of Cryptozoology* was one of the American Library Association's Outstanding Reference Works in 2006. His nonfiction work includes numerous volumes for Chelsea House Publishers and Facts On File.